Photon

**Written by Wallie Winholtz,
Kathy Cramer, Sherry Twyman,
& B. K. Hixson**

Photon U

Copyright © 2001
First Printing • January 2001
B. K. Hixson

Published by Loose in the Lab, Inc.
9462 South 560 West
Sandy, Utah 84070

www.looseinthelab.com

Library of Congress Cataloging-in-Publication Data:

Hixson, B. K.
     Photon U / B. K. Hixson, Wallie Winholtz, Kathy
Cramer, & Sherry Twyman
         p.   cm.-(Loose in the Lab Science Series)

     Includes glossary and index
     ISBN 0-9660965-5-x
  1. Visual perception-experiments-juvenile literature.
[1. Visual perception-Experiments   2. Experiments]
I.Wallie Winholtz II. Kathy Cramer III. Sherry Twyman
IV. Loose in the Lab V. Title VI. Series
QP441.D54   2000
152.14

Printed in the United States of America
Let there be light!

Dedication

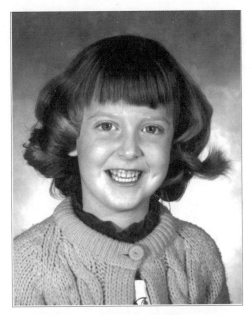

Marjorie Ann Hixson
(Kindergarten Princess, Circa 1973)

For my little sis, all grown up, who loves light, texture, color, form, and shape. You have a great gift for taking these abstractions and producing wonderful things with them. I am delighted whenever you share.

For all the times I noogied your noggin, rolled you in the mud, licked your eyelids, and generally behaved in the characteristic manner of an older (and wiser) big brother I both humbly apologize and fully recognize that it is now your privilege and honor as "Aunt" to incur the same on your nieces and nephew. If you want help catching them, let me know. Oh, and nice hairdo. Did Dad get you ready for school that morning?

Hugs & Kisses,

♡ Bryce

Acknowledgments

There are always a lot of thank-yous that need to be passed out when a book gets published, and this one is no exception. On top of the list are my co-authors Wallie Winholtz, Kathy Cramer, and Sherry Twyman, the infamous Missouri Gang, a cadre of middle school teachers from Kansas City who submitted the basic ideas that provided the foundation for this book. Their complete works can be found in two teacher-oriented resource books titled *Roy Boy & The Amazing Technicolor Wind Sock* (Grades 2–3) and *The Electromagnetic ZapPak* (Grades 5–6).

As for my educational outlook (the hands-on perspective and the use of humor in the classroom), Dr. Fox, my senior professor at Oregon State University, gets the credit for shaping my educational philosophy recognizing that even at the collegiate level we were on to something a little different. He did his very best to encourage, nurture, and support me while I was getting basket loads of opposition for being willing to swim upstream. Also several colleagues did their very best to channel my enthusiasm during those early, formative years of teaching: Dick Bishop, Dick Hinton, Dee Strange, and Linda Zimmermann. Thanks for your patience, friendship, and support.

Next up are all the folks that get to do the dirty work that make the final publication look so polished but very rarely get the credit they deserve. Next, our resident graphics guru/web-head, Ed Seghini gets a nod for scanning and cleaning the artwork that you find on these pages as well as putting together the graphics that make up the cover. All of that is done so that Kathleen Hixson and Diane Burns can take turns simultaneously proofreading the text while mocking my writing skills. Only then is the manuscript handed over to Susan Moore who peruses it with her scanning electon microscope eyes and adds hyphens, commas, capitals, and other formal genera of the grammatical world that have eluded me for decades.

Once the finished product is done, the book has to be printed by the good folks at Advanced Graphics—Michael Williams, Matt and the crew, so that Stefan Kohler, Louisa Walker, and the Delta Education gang can market, ship the books, collect the money, and send us a couple of nickels. A short thank-you, for a couple of very important jobs.

Mom and Dad, as always, get the end credits. Thanks for the education, encouragement, and love. And for Kathy and the kids—Porter, Shelby, Courtney, and Aubrey—hugs and kisses.

Repro Rights

There is very little about this book that is truly formal, but at the insistence of our wise and esteemed counsel, let us declare: *No part of this book may be reproduced or utilized in any form or by any means, electronic or mechanical, including photocopying, recording, or by any information storage and retrieval system, without permission in writing from the publisher.* That would be us.

More Legal Stuff

Official disclaimer for you aspiring scientists and lab groupies. This is a hands-on science book. By the very intent of the design, you will be directed to use common, nontoxic, household items in a safe and responsible manner to avoid injury to yourself and others who are present while you are pursuing your quest for knowledge and enlightenment in the world of physics. Praise the Almighty and pass the hologram.

If, for some reason, perhaps even beyond your own control, you have an affinity for disaster, we wish you well. *But we, in no way take any responsibility for any injury that is incurred to any person using the information provided in this book or for any damage to personal property or effects that are directly or indirectly a result of the suggested activities contained herein.* Translation: You're on your own. Even James Bond knew that he was no match for a good old-fashioned laser.

Less Formal Legal Stuff

If you are in need of further clarification or simply choose to ignore this pleasant and polite caution, we will send Kim Chee, our garlic-snarfing personal trainer, to your address. She, in turn, will exhale in your general direction a repeated number of times until you succumb to the haze of fermented cabbage and partially decomposed oriental vegetables. If that does not work, then we will turn our legal counsel loose on you. Guaranteed not to be a pretty sight for onlookers, unless you enjoy those nature movies that feature carnivorous attacks on diseased range animals.

Table of Contents

The National Content Standards (Grades K–4)

Light travels in a straight line until it strikes an object. Light can be reflected by a mirror, refracted by a lens, or absorbed by the object.

The National Content Standards (Grades 5–8)

Light interacts with matter (including refraction) absorption, or scattering (including reflection). To see an object, light from that object, emitted by or scattered from it, must enter the eye.

The 15 Big Ideas About Light & Corresponding Labs

1. Visible light is a form of energy that makes up a very small portion of the electromagnetic spectrum. This light energy can be measured and then described using the terms *wave, crest, trough, amplitude,* and *frequency.*

2. We can detect light using our eyes. The human eye can be described using several different models to demonstrate how the different parts function.

3. Organelles called cones and rods collect the light images that enter the eye and transmit them to the brain. Their presence in the eye also creates other phenomena we can detect.

4. White light is composed of all the colors of the rainbow: red, orange, yellow, green, blue, indigo, and violet. White light can be separated into all of these colors when it passes through a prism or diffraction grating.

5. Red, blue, and yellow are the primary colors of the rainbow. These three colors can be mixed in a variety of combinations and produce all of the other colors that we see.

6. When light strikes an object, it can be completely reflected or absorbed, diffused, or transmitted. The terms used to describe these phenomena are *opaque, translucent,* and *transparent.*

7. Light emitted from different materials can be filtered and observed through a diffraction grating to produce characteristic patterns that are unique to that material. These patterns, or fingerprints, of light can be used to identify different kinds of materials.

Even More Contents

8. White light can be polarized using a special filter that allows certain wavelengths of light to pass through while blocking others.

9. A lens is a tool that is used to bend, diffuse, magnify, or concentrate light. It can be made of glass, plastic, water, and other transparent materials.

10. Light can be bent as it passes through certain materials. The amount it is bent is called the index of refraction and varies from material to material.

11. Light can be reflected off the surface of a material. The incident angle of light always equals the reflected angle of light.

12. Light can enter and be completely reflected inside some objects. When this phenomenon happens, it is called total internal reflection.

13. Waves can bounce off surfaces and interfere with other light waves. This is called wave interference, which can be either constructive or destructive.

14. Optical illusions are light images that are reflected to the eye and trick the brain into thinking it is seeing something it is not.

15. Light can be absorbed. When this happens, the object that absorbs the light may experience a temperature increase, color change, or possibly a change of state.

Who Are You ? And ...

First of all, we may have an emergency at hand and we'll both want to cut to the chase and get the patient into the cardiac unit if necessary. So, before we go too much further, **define yourself**. Please check one and only one choice listed below and then immediately follow the directions that follow *in italics*. Thank you in advance for your cooperation.

I am holding this book because. . .

_____ **A. I am a responsible, but panicked, parent.** My son/daughter/triplets (circle one) just informed me that his/her/their science fair project is due tomorrow. This is the only therapy I could afford on such short notice. Which means that if I was not holding this book, my hands would be encircling the soon-to-be-worm-bait's neck.

Directions: Can't say this is the first or the last time we heard that one. Hang in there, we can do this.

1. Quickly read the Table of Contents with the worm bait. The Big Ideas define what each section is about. Obviously, the kid is not passionate about science, or you would not be in this situation. See if you can find an idea that causes some portion of an eyelid or facial muscle to twitch.

If that does not work, we recommend narrowing the list to the following labs because they are fast, use materials that can be acquired with limited notice, and the intrinsic level of interest is generally quite high.

How to Use This Book

2. *Take the materials list from the lab write-up and from page 193 of the Surviving a Science Fair Project section and go shopping.*

3. *Assemble the materials and perform the lab at least once. Gather as much data as you can.*

4. *Go to page 170 and read the material. Then start on Step 1 of Preparing Your Science Fair Project. With any luck you can dodge an academic disaster.*

___ **B. I am worm bait.** My science fair project is due tomorrow, and there is not anything moldy in the fridge. I need a big Band-Aid™, in a hurry.

Directions: Same as Option A. You can decide if and when you want to clue your folks in on your current dilemma.

___ **C. I am the parent of a student who informed me that he/she has been assigned a science fair project due in six to eight weeks.** My son/daughter has expressed an interest in science books with humorous illustrations that attempt to explain light and associated phenomena.

Who Are You ? And ...

Directions: Well, you came to the right place. Give your kid these directions and stand back.

1. The first step is to read through the Table of Contents and see if anything grabs your interest. Read through several experiments, see if the science teacher has any of the more difficult materials to acquire like diffraction gratings, polarizing filters, and some of the chemicals, and ask if they can be borrowed. Play with the experiments and see which one really tickles your fancy.

2. After you have found and conducted an experiment that you like, take a peek at the Science Fair Ideas and see if you would like to investigate one of those or create an idea of your own. The guidelines for those are listed on page 182 in the Surviving Your Science Fair section. You have plenty of time so you can fiddle and fool with the original experiment and its derivations several times. Work until you have an original question you want to answer and then start the process, listed on page 182. You are well on your way to an excellent grade.

___ D. I am a responsible student and have been assigned a science fair project due in six to eight weeks. I am interested in light, and despite demonstrating maturity and wisdom well beyond the scope of my peers, I too still have a sense of humor. Enlighten and entertain me.

Directions: Cool. Being teachers, we have heard reports of this kind of thing happening but usually in an obscure and hard-to-locate town several states removed. Nonetheless, congratulations.

Same as Option C. You have plenty of time and should be able to score very well. We'll keep our eyes peeled when the Nobel Prizes are announced in a couple of years.

How to Use This Book

___ E. I am a parent who home schools my child/children. We are always on the lookout for quality curriculum materials that are not only educationally sound but also kid- and teacher-friendly. I am not particularly strong in science, but I realize it is a very important topic. How is this book going to help me out?

Directions: In a lot of ways we created this book specifically for home schoolers.

1. We have taken the National Content Standards, the guidelines that are used by all public and private schools nationwide to establish their curriculum base, and listed them in the Table of Contents. You now know where you stand with respect to the national standards.

2. We then break these standards down and list the major ideas that you should want your kid to know. We call these the Big Ideas. Some people call them objectives, others call them curriculum standards, educational benchmarks, or assessment norms. Same apple, different name. The bottom line is that when your child is done studying this unit on light you want them not only to understand and explain each of the 15 Big Ideas listed in this book, but also, to be able to defend and argue their position based on experiential evidence that they have collected.

3. Building on the Big Ideas, we have collected and rewritten 50 hands-on science labs. Each one has been specifically selected so that it supports the Big Idea that it is correlated to. This is critical. As the kids do the science experiment, they see, smell, touch, and hear the experiment. They will store that information in several places in their brains. When it comes time to comprehend the Big Idea, the concrete hands-on experiences provide the foundation for building the Idea, which is quite often abstract. Kids who merely read about diffraction gratings, polarizing filters, and optical illusions, or who see pictures of the model of an eye or inverted images created by pinhole cameras are trying to build abstract ideas on abstract ideas and quite often miss the mark.

Who Are You ? And ...

*For example: I can show you a recipe in a book for chocolate chip cookies and ask you to reiterate it. Or I can turn you loose in a kitchen, have you mix the ingredients, grease the pan, plop the dough on the cookie sheet, slide everything into the oven, and wait impatiently until they pop out eight minutes later. Chances are that the description given by the person who actually made the cookies is going to be much clearer because it is based on their true understanding of the process, **because it is based on experience.***

4. Once you have completed the experiment, there are a number of extension ideas under the Science Fair Extensions that allow you to spend as much or as little time on the ideas as you deem necessary.

5. A word about humor. Science is not usually known for being funny even though Bill Nye, The Science Guy, *Beaker from* Sesame Street, *and* Beakman's World *do their best to mingle the two. That's all fine and dandy, but we want you to know that we incorporate humor because it is scientifically (and educationally) sound to do so. Plus it's really at the root of our personalities. Here's what we know:*

When we laugh ...
a. Our pupils dilate, increasing the amount of light entering the eye.
b. Our heart rate increases, which pumps more blood to the brain.
c. Oxygen-rich blood to the brain means the brain is able to collect, process, and store more information. Big I.E.: increased comprehension.
d. Laughter relaxes muscles, which can be involuntarily tense if a student is uncomfortable or fearful of an academic topic.
e. Laughter stimulates the immune system, which will ultimately translate into overall health and fewer kids who say they are sick of science.
f. Socially, it provides an acceptable pause in the academic routine, which then gives the student time to regroup and prepare to address some of the more difficult ideas with a renewed spirit. They can study longer and focus on ideas more efficiently.
g. Laughter releases chemicals in the brain that are associated with pleasure and joy.
6. If you follow the book in the order it is written, you will be able to build ideas and concepts in a logical and sequential pattern. But that is by no means necessary. For a complete set of guidelines on our ideas on how to teach home-schooled kids science, check out our book, Why's the Cat on Fire? How to Excel at Teaching Science to Your Home-Schooled Kids.

How to Use This Book

___ F. **I am a public/private school teacher,** and this looks like an interesting book to add ideas to my classroom lesson plans.

Directions: It is, and please feel free to do so. However, while this is a great classroom resource for kids, may we also recommend two other titles The Electromagnetic ZapPak *if you wish to teach light to fourth through sixth graders and* Roy Boy & the Amazing Technicolor Wind Sock *for the K–3 range.*

These two books have teacher-preparation pages, student-response sheets or lab pages, lesson plans, bulletin board ideas, discovery center ideas, vocabulary sheets, unit pretests, unit exams, lab practical exams, and student grading sheets. Basically everything you need if you are a science nincompoop, and a couple of cool ideas if you are a seasoned veteran with an established curriculum. All of the ideas that are covered in this one book are covered much more thoroughly in the other two. They were specifically written for teachers.

___ G. **My son/daughter/grandson/niece/father-in-law** is interested in science, and this looks like fun.

Directions: Congratulations on your selection. Add a gift certificate to the local science supply store and a package of hot chocolate mix and you have the perfect rainy Saturday afternoon gig.

___ H. **My gardening club** has been talking about the effect of filtered radiant light on the photosynthetic process with respect to alternating energy levels as a function of solar prominences. We were wondering if you could help us out.

Directions: Nope. Try the university.

Lab Safety

Contained herein are 50 science activities to help you better understand the nature and characteristics of light as we currently understand these things. However, since you are on your own in this journey we thought it prudent to share some basic wisdom and experience in the safety department.

Read the Instructions

An interesting concept, especially if you are a teenager. Take a minute before you jump in and get going to read all of the instructions as well as warnings. If you do not understand something, stop and ask an adult for help.

Clean Up All Messes

Keep your lab area clean. It will make it easier to put everything away at the end and may also prevent contamination and the subsequent germination of a species of mutant tomato bug larva. You will also find that chemicals perform with more predictability if they are not poisoned with foreign molecules.

Organize

Translation: Put it back where you get it. If you need any more clarification, there is an opening at the landfill for you.

Dispose of Poisons Properly

This will not be much of a problem with labs that use, study, split, and mix light. However, if you happen to wander over into one of the many disciplines that incorporates the use of chemicals, then we would suggest that you use great caution with the materials and definitely dispose of any and all poisons properly.

Practice Good Fire Safety

If there is a fire in the room, notify an adult immediately. If an adult is not in the room and the fire is manageable, smother the outbreak with a fire blanket or use a fire extinguisher. When the fire is contained, immediately send someone to find an adult.

If, for any reason, you happen to catch on fire, **REMEMBER: Stop, Drop, and Roll.** Never run; it adds oxygen to the fire, making it burn faster, and it also scares the bat guano out of the neighbors when they see the neighbor kids running down the block doing an imitation of a campfire marshmallow without the stick.

Protect Your Skin

It is a good idea to always wear protective gloves whenever you are working with chemicals. Again, this particular book does not suggest or incorporate chemicals in its lab activities very often. However, when we do, we are incorporating only safe, manageable kinds of chemicals for these labs. If you do happen to spill a chemical on your skin, notify an adult immediately and then flush the area with water for 15 minutes. It's unlikely, but if irritation develops, have your parents or another responsible adult look at it. If it appears to be of concern, contact a physician. Take any information that you have about the chemical with you.

Lab Safety

Save Your Nose Hairs

Sounds like a cause celebre LA style, but it is really good advice. To smell a chemical to identify it, hold the open container six to ten inches down and away from your nose. Make a clockwise circular motion with your hand over the opening of the container, "wafting" some of the fumes toward your nose. This will allow you to safely smell some of the fumes without exposing youself to a large dose of anything noxious. This technique may help prevent a nosebleed or your lungs from accidentally getting burned by chemicals.

Wear Goggles If Appropriate

If the lab asks you to heat or mix chemicals, be sure to wear protective eyewear. Also have an eyewash station or running water available. You never know when something is going to splatter, splash, or react unexpectedly. It is better to look like a nerd and be prepared than schedule a trip down to pick out a Seeing Eye™ dog. If you do happen to accidentally get chemicals in your eye, flush the area for 15 minutes. If any irritation or pain develops, immediately go see a doctor.

Lose the Comedy Routine

You should have plenty of time scheduled during your day to mess around, but science lab is not one of them. Horseplay breaks glassware, spills chemicals, and creates unnecessary messes—things that parents do not appreciate. Trust us on this one.

No Eating

Do not eat while performing a lab. Putting your food in the lab area contaminates your food and the experiment. This makes for bad science and worse indigestion. Avoid poisoning yourself and goobering up your lab ware by observing this rule.

Happy and safe experimenting!

Recommended Materials Suppliers

For every lesson in this book we offer a list of materials. Many of these are very easy to acquire, and if you do not have them in your home already, you will be able to find them at the local grocery or hardware store. For more difficult items we have selected, for your convenience, a small but respectable list of suppliers who will meet your needs in a timely and economical manner. Call for a catalog or quote on the item that you are looking for, and they will be happy to give you a hand.

Loose in the Lab
9462 South 560 West
Sandy, Utah 84070
Phone 1-888-403-1189
Fax 1-801-568-9586
www.looseinthelab.com

Delta Education
80 NW Boulevard
Nashua, NH 03601
Phone 1-800-442-5444
Fax 1-800-282-9560
www.delta-ed.com

Nasco
901 Jonesville Ave.
Fort Atkinson, Wisconsin 53538
Phone 1-414-563-2446
Fax 1-920-563-8296
www.nascofa.com

Ward's Scientific
5100 W Henrietta Road
Rochester, New York 14692
Phone 800-387-7822
Fax 1-716-334-6174
www.wardsci.com

Educational Innovations
151 River Road
Cos Cob, Conneticut 06807
Phone 1-888-912-7474
Fax 1-203-629-2739
www.teachersource.com

Frey Scientific
100 Paragon Parkway
Mansfield, Ohio 44903
Phone 1-800-225-FREY
Fax 1-419-589-1546
www.freyscientific.com

Edmund Scientific
101 E. Gloucester Pike
Barrington, NJ 08007
Phone 1-(800) 728-6999
Fax 1-856-547-3292
www.edmundscientific.com

Sargent Welch Scientific Co.
911 Commerce Court
Buffalo Grove, Illinois 60089
Phone 800-727-4368
Fax 1-800-676-2540
www.sargentwelch.com

The Ideas, Lab Activities, & Science Fair Extensions

Big Idea 1

Visible light is a form of energy that makes up a very small portion of the electromagnetic spectrum.

This light energy can be measured and then described using the terms *wave, crest, trough, frequency,* and *amplitude.*

Stretching Rainbows

The Experiment

There are all kinds of waves out there: X rays, gamma rays, cosmic rays, ultraviolet rays, radio waves, television waves, and the colors we see called visible light rays. If you could see these waves, they would look like a series of sideways S's that are all connected together. We are going to cover the very basics in this lab.

Scientists measure different kinds of waves and use these measurements to classify them. Before we get into the measuring of waves, we need to give the different parts names. A complete wave is pictured to the right. The top of the wave is called the *crest*, the bottom of the wave is the *trough*. One complete cycle, up and down, is considered a *wave*.

The waves are measured two ways. First, they measure one complete sideways S. This is called the *frequency*. Take a centimeter. If one wave (a complete sideways S) fits perfectly in that distance, the frequency of that wave is measured at one wave per centimeter or 1 centimeter. If two waves fit in the same distance, the frequency is now .5 centimeter. The higher the frequency, the tighter the S's are packed together and the more waves you can squish into a space.

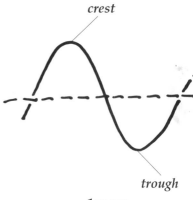

crest

trough

1 wave

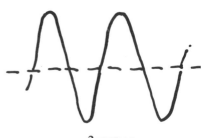

2 waves
higher frequency

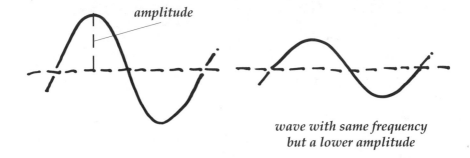

amplitude

wave with same frequency but a lower amplitude

The other measurement that is important is the *amplitude*. The amplitude is how high the S stretches up and down. For music waves the amplitude is directly correlated to the loudness of the music. You can blow the same note into a trumpet over and over, and it will always vibrate at the same frequency. If you blow hard and produce a loud tone, it changes the amplitude but not the frequency. If you blow softly, the amplitude is smaller, but the frequency is exactly the same.

This lab is going to allow you to "collect" a sample of each of the visible rays, stretch them out, and compare the amount of energy that each one carries with it as it travels through space.

Materials
1 Pair of Scissors
1 Metric Ruler
1 Spool of Thread of each of the following colors:
      red, orange, yellow, green, blue, indigo
1 Wave Diagram, found on page 24

Procedure
1. To determine the amount of energy that is in a wave, we are going to take the wave, stretch it out, and measure it.

2. On the next page are the colors of the rainbow drawn as actual frequencies. Your job is to measure each of them using a length of colored thread. To do this you start with the red frequency and lay the red thread along all of the waves shown on each of the lines. Match it as closely as you can and cut the thread at the end of each wave. Measure the length and enter that information in the data table.

Stretching Rainbows

3. Repeat this procedure for all of the colors.

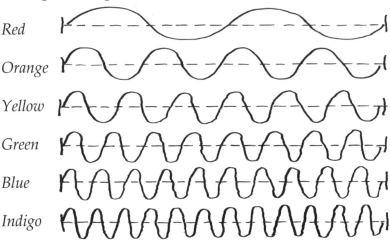

Red

Orange

Yellow

Green

Blue

Indigo

Data & Observations

Color	Wavelengths
Red	
Orange	
Yellow	
Green	
Blue	
Indigo	

How Come, Huh?

The length of the thread represents the amount of energy stored in each wavelength. As you can see by the measurement, blue/indigo wavelengths have more energy (they are longer) than red/orange waves.

Talc Beams

The Experiment

You cannot see light unless you look directly at the source, or the light waves reflect off a surface to your eye. You will demonstrate this by shooting a single beam of light across a dark room. You won't be able to see the light until you reveal it, using talcum powder.

Materials

1   Index Card
1   Hole Punch
1   Flashlight
1   Roll of Tape
1   Bottle of Talcum Powder
1   Dark Room

CARD W/ HOLE

TAPE

Procedure

1. Using the hole punch make a hole in the center of the index card.

2. Tape the index card to the front of a flashlight so that the bulb is lined up directly with the hole in the card.

3. Darken the room and turn the flashlight on. Shine the light around the room and try to see the beam—not the dot of light reflecting off the wall, chair, desk, or other object, but the actual beam. You can't.

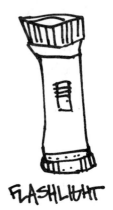

FLASHLIGHT

4. Holding the flashlight parallel to the ground or placing it on a table top to keep it steady, sprinkle a small amount of talcum powder where the beam of light appears to be shining. If your guess is correct, the beam will appear.

Talc Beams

How Come, Huh?

Light cannot be seen unless it is viewed directly at the source or is reflected off a surface to our eyes. In this case, the beam zipped through the darkened room undetected until it hit the wall or some other object and was

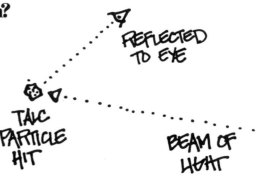

reflected to your eye. When you sprinkled talcum powder, the air was filled full of little obstacles that reflected light to your eyes. As the zillions of particles of light traveled through the beam, many of them collided with the talcum powder and some were reflected to your eye.

Science Fair Extensions

1. Arrange a series of mirrors so they are lined up to bounce light from one to another. Turn the lights off and the flashlight on. The beams of light traveling between the mirrors will be invisible until you walk around the room sprinkling talcum powder to reveal the light beams. This technique is used in a lot of spy and thief movies to reveal laser security beams crisscrossing the floors of museums and high tech factories.

2. Figure out what other materials you can use to reveal a beam of light. Be sure to ask your mom before you start sprinkling baking soda and powdered sugar on the kitchen floor.

Big Idea 2

We can detect light using our eyes. The human eye can be described by using several different models to demonstrate how the different parts function.

Fishbowl Lens

The Experiment

Fishbowls, like the ones that you can win full of goldfish at the state or county fair, are shaped roughly like our eyes. You can also find lightbulb covers that are the same shape. When either of these are filled with water, they can be used to bend and focus light.

Materials

1   Glass Sphere
    Water
1   Votive Candle
1   Book of Matches
1   Index Card
1   Metric Ruler
1   Dark Room

Procedure

1. Fill the sphere completely with water and place it in front of you on the table.

2. With the assistance or supervision of an adult, light the candle and darken the room.

3. Place the candle on one side of the sphere, about 8 inches away. Place the index card on the other side of the sphere, also about 8 inches away, so that they are all in a straight line.

4. You should see an inverted (upside down) image of the candle flame projected on the card. Experiment with moving the index card toward and away from the glass sphere until the image of the flame is in focus.

5. Experiment and fill in the data table on the next page.

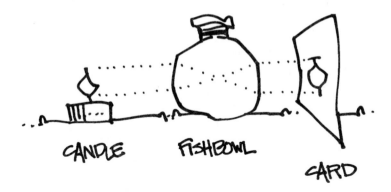

CANDLE   FISHBOWL

CARD

Data & Observations

Measure from the center of the bowl to the center of the candle to set the first variable of the experiment. Next measure from the center of the bowl to the index card and record the results in the table.

Candle to Bowl Distance (cm)	Index Card to Bowl Distance (cm)
10 cm	
15 cm	
20 cm	
25 cm	

How Come, Huh?

The bowl acts like a giant convex lens. As the image of the candle strikes the glass, it bends. It bends again as it travels through the water; then it bends one more time as it leaves the water and goes through the glass into the air. The illustration at the top of the page should help a little.

Science Fair Extensions

3. Substitute different liquids for the water and see if it affects the focal distance or the size of the image.

4. Try this experiment using a bowl full of air.

Camera in a Cup

The Experiment

This experiment gives you the opportunity to see how a camera works. You are going to assemble a very simple device that will collect the light emitted from a candle flame and project it onto a sheet of wax paper. Upside down, just as you might, or might not, expect.

Materials

1   Dark Room
1   Paper Clip
1   5 oz. Wax Cup
1   6" by 6" Sheet of Wax Paper
1   Rubber Band
1   Votive Candle
1   Book of Matches

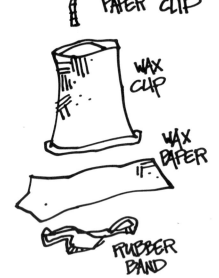

PAPER CLIP

WAX CUP

WAX PAPER

RUBBER BAND

Procedure

1. Open the paper clip and punch a small hole in the bottom of the wax cup.

2. Fold the wax paper over the open end of the cup and secure it with the rubber band. You are now in possession of a very, very simple camera.

3. Darken the room and light the candle. Hold the cup so that the small hole in the bottom is pointing toward the candle flame. Looking at the wax paper end of your camera, move the cup back and forth until the image of the candle flame is a clear, sharp image on the wax paper.

How Come, Huh?

The light traveling from the candle is moving in a straight line. The illustration shows the rays of light from the candle crisscross as they enter the hole. This creates the inverted, or upside down, image you see on the wax paper.

INVERTED IMAGE

Science Fair Extensions

5. Keep the wax cup in the same place and move the candle flame horizontally and vertically. Write a "law" that describes the motion of the image and draw pictures of why this happens.

6. Experiment with different sizes of cups, toilet paper tubes, or small boxes. Determine the focal length for each one. See if there is a common denominator or formula that you can derive from your measurements to be able to predict the focal length for any given "camera" that you make.

7. With the permission of a supervising adult, turn an entire room into a camera. Find a room that has a window to the outside. Cover all of the windows with black paper, leaving one small hole the size of a quarter in the center of one window. Darken the entire room and then instruct your mom, a sister, or someone to walk by the window. As they pass by the small hole that is allowing light into the room, their inverted image should be projected on to the opposite wall. You are *inside* a giant camera!

Eyeballoon Models

The Experiment

You are going to create a simple model of an eyeball, affectionately known as "the eyeballoon." In doing so, you will begin to understand how we see the world around us. The exact mechanics of how the brain actually "sees" remains a mystery, but we have a good idea of how the light reaches the gray matter that we haul around inside our skull.

Our eyes work in many ways like a camera. Light enters through a lens, and the image produced comes from many parts working together. This setup will provide a good working model.

Materials

1   Biconvex Plastic Lens
1   White, 9", Round Balloon
1   Assistant
1   Votive Candle
1   Black Marker
1   Book of Matches
1   Metric Ruler

Procedure

1. Inflate your balloon to approximately the size of a huge grapefruit or a smallish canteloupe. If you have trouble blowing the balloon up, stretch it a couple of times to loosen the rubber and try again. If you are still having a hard time, ask for assistance from an adult or older sibling.

2. You are going to want to work with someone for this step. While your partner pinches the neck of the balloon to prevent air from escaping, insert the lens into the opening of the balloon. The lens, when it is in place, should be perpendicular to the neck of the balloon. Use the illustration above as a guide. You will not need to tie the balloon off to prevent air from escaping.

Like your eye, you want light to enter the lens and travel through the balloon so that it hits the back of the balloon. Feel free to use the marker to add eyelashes, blood vessels, and so on.

3. Hold the eye balloon in one hand with the opening of the balloon and the lens pointing toward you. Grab the lens between your thumb and forefinger and stare right through the lens and into the center of the balloon. You should have a clear, unimpeded view. Give the balloon half a twist. The neck of the balloon gets smaller and smaller until it closes, much like the aperture of a single lens reflex camera and the pupils of your own eyes. Experiment with opening and closing the pupils. We'll cover more on this function on page 48.

4. With the supervision of an adult, light the candle and darken the room.

CANDLE   BALLOON

IMAGE OF FLAME

Eyeballoon Models

5.   Place your eyeballoon on the table between you and the candle with the lens pointed toward the candle flame, which should be approximately 20 to 30 cm away. Use the illustration as a guide. You should be able to see the image of the candle flame projected onto the rubber surface at the back of the balloon. Slowly move the balloon forward and backward until you are able to "focus" the image of the flame on the back of the balloon, and it is very clear and bright. When your balloon is in focus, proceed to the Data, Observations, & Questions Section and start collecting data.

CANDLE   BALLOON

Data, Observations, & Questions

1. Draw a picture of how the candle flame appears on the back of the rubber balloon. Use the space below.

2. Describe how the image of the flame you see on the back of the balloon is different from the image of the flame you see with your eyes.

_____

_____

_____

_____.

3. The distance from the center of the flame on the candle to the image projected on the back of the balloon is called the focal length. Measure and record that distance in the space below.

Focal Length: _____ cm

CANDLE   HAND 1   HAND 2

Sometimes the muscles that are attached to the eye will pull the eye out of its normal position. Try pushing gently down from the top of the eyeballoon, making the eyeballoon short and fat.

4. How does this affect the candle image that you see on the back of the balloon? This approximates the effect that a nearsighted person experiences.

_____

_____

_____

_____

Eyeballoon Models

5. Repeat step four, but gently push in from the front and the back making the eyeballoon tall. What effect does this have on the image you see? This approximates the effect that a farsighted person experiences.

_____

_____

_____.

How Come, Huh?

Let's slice your eye apart, one section at a time:

1. The white part of the balloon represents the white part of the eye called the sclera. This is the protein coating that surrounds the vitreous humor, lens, and ciliary muscles, and holds the whole sphere together. This is the part of your eye that your mother is so concerned about when she tells you not to play with sharp sticks or "Someone could lose an eye!" You won't lose your eye, but if you puncture your sclera, the vitreous humor will leak out of your eye and the lens could fall away from the pupil. Might as well have lost the eye at this point.

2. When the plastic lens was inserted into the neck of the balloon, it represented the lens that we have in each eye. The rubber around the lens represents the ciliary muscles that are part of the iris. This controls the amount of light that enters the eye. The iris of the eye acts in the same manner as the iris of a camera. When it is dark, the iris is more open, and when it is bright, the iris closes to reduce the amount of light and protect the tissue.

3. The inside back of the balloon is similar to the retina. It supports the cones and rods, which collect and send the light information to the brain.

4. . . . and the eyelashes were probably just like Miss Maybelline. Sorry, had to see if you were paying attention.

5. When the balloon was focused on the candle, you were determining the focal length of a "normal" eye. By squishing the balloon and creating the "Fat Eye," you were creating the condition that exists in the human eye that causes nearsightedness. The eyeball becomes distorted, and the focal point of the lens places the image somewhere in front of the retina so things look blurry. The "Tall Eye" is a model for farsightedness. The image is actually focused beyond the back of the eye, and these people have exceptionally good vision over distances but tend to have a harder time with things that are up close.

Science Fair Extensions

8. Experiment with adding additional lenses to correct for the near- and farsighted balloons. Determine the distance, and the kind of lens that needs to be placed in front of the lens in the balloon to correct the vision.

9. Dissect a preserved cow or sheep eye. Compare the actual anatomy found in a once-living, eye with the model that is created in the eyeballoon lab. How are they similar? What makes them different?

10. Compare the way that a single lens reflex camera operates to the way our eyes function. Find an old, dead camera and dissect it, showing the different parts and comparing them to the living tissue.

Sheep Eye Scallopini

The Experiment

We are going to take the bulk of the lab investigating a sheep eye. The eye has been preserved in a chemical that prevents decomposition. It is not poisonous, but you will want to wear latex gloves at all times. Ask an adult to make the preliminary cut, you can do the rest.

Materials

1   Cow Eye
1   Dissecting Probe
1   Pair of Dissecting Scissors
1   Pair of Gloves
1   Garbage Can
1   Roll of Paper Towels

Procedure

1. Trim the fat and muscle away from the sheep eye. There will be a hard, round, white, thick cord attached to the back of the eye. This is the optic nerve. It carries the information from the eye to the brain. Do not cut this, just trim away most of the excess.

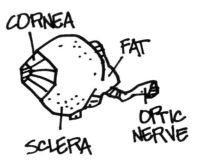

2. Once the muscle and fat have been removed, ask an adult to cut the eye in half for you. The white part of the eye is called the sclera. Remove the lens, which will be connected to the ciliary muscles and vitreous humor, and set it aside.

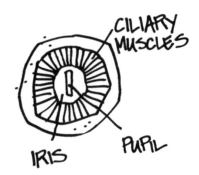

3. Separate the eye into two equal halves. The front half of the eye contains the pupil (the hole) in the iris. The colored part of the eye is the iris, and the sectioned, black fibers are called the ciliary muscles. They are responsible for manipulating the pupil.

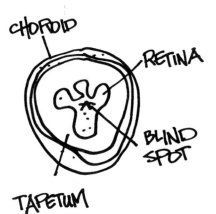

4. The back half of the eye contains a light-colored blob. This is the retina. The pucker in the middle is the blind spot where the optic nerve is attached. The bluish black coating is called the tapetum and is found only in some animals. It reflects some of the light

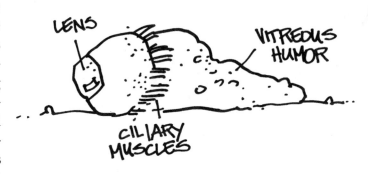

back out through the pupil. This is what gives cats and dogs those glow-in-the-dark eyes late at night when headlights shine in their eyes. The choroid is directly under the tapetum and supports it.

5. When you cut the eye in half, there is a good chance that the lens fell out of the eye. It will look cloudy and yellow. This is not the natural state of the lens, but what happens when it is soaked in a preservative. The lens focuses the light that enters the eyeball. It will be attached to the vitreous humor by the thin, black ciliary muscles. The vitreous humor fills the sclera and gives the eye shape. This is one of the reasons your mom tells you not to play with sticks. If you poke your eye, the vitreous humor oozes out and the lens falls away.

Sheep Eye Scallopini

Data & Observations

Draw pictures of the parts of the eye listed below each box.

The eye right out of the package. Side view	*The eye right out of the package. Front view*	*The inside of the eye, looking at the pupil*

The inside of the eye, looking at the blind spot	*The lens attached to the ciliary muscles, et al*	*The look on your mother's face when you showed the eye to her*

Science Fair Extensions

11. Go to the local meat-processing plant or butcher shop and see if you can find a diseased cow or sheep eye to dissect and compare with the healthy eye. Identify the differences in your dissection.

12. Make a scale model of an eye using the eye that you dissected as a guide. Show how you took the measurements to build the model to scale.

Big Idea 3

Organelles called cones and rods collect the light images that enter the eye and transmit them to the brain. Their presence in the eye also creates other phenomena we can detect.

Peripheral Vision

The Experiment

Rods and cones refer to many things, but most folks wouldn't guess they are part of your eye. They turn the light that comes into the eye into an image. From peripheral vision, to colors, to detailed shapes, the cones and rods are part of the team that gets the job done. This experiment measures your peripheral vision with a simple device.

Materials

1   Piece of String, 60 cm. long
1   Pair of Scissors
1   Pencil
1   30 x 60 cm. Piece of Cardboard
1   Pushpin
1   Protractor (find on page 215 of this book)
1   Bottle of White Glue
1   Piece of Blank Paper
5   Different Colored Markers
1   5 oz. Wax Cup
1   Assistant

Procedure

1. Tie the string to the pencil using the illustration to the right as a guide. Shove a pushpin into the edge of the cardboard sheet. Tie the other end of the string around the pushpin.

2. Use the pencil, string, and pushpin to draw a half-circle on your cardboard with the radius of 30 cm. Cut this half-circle out. Repeat this step using a 2 cm. radius and cut it out. This will be the nose position. Use the illustration at the top of the next page as a guide.

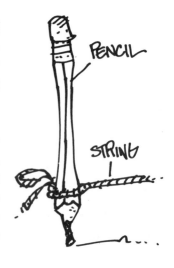

PENCIL

STRING

3. In the very back of this book there is a protractor that you can photocopy, cut out, and use to measure the angles of the bouncing light. You can also use a commercial protractor available where school supplies are sold.

4. Lay the half-circle out before you and insert a "focus pin" across from the smaller "nose position" notch. To do this, simply stick your pushpin into the cardboard, close to the edge, opposite the nose position.

5. Laying a protractor over the nose cutout, mark the edge of the card board sheet in increments of 5 degrees on both sides of the focal pin. You will use these measurements to determine the peripheral vision of your lab assistants.

6. Take the 5 oz. wax cup and run a line of glue around the drinking edge. Stick this to the underside of your semicircle. This will be a handle by which to hold your peripheral vision measuring contraption. Allow plenty of time to dry!

FOCUS PIN

CUP HANDLE

Peripheral Vision

7. With the blank sheet of paper, fold over approximately 3 cm or 1 inch starting from any side. Continue folding over and over until you have reached the other side. At the top and bottom of the front and back draw a different shape and color. For example, a red triangle on one side and a blue square on the other. Use the other end (front and back) and draw a green circle on one side and a yellow octagon on the back. This is known as the shape stick.

8. When the handle (cup) has dried, hold the cup and bring the whole cardboard semicircle up to and straight out from your nose, as if you were looking across your desk at "eye level." Focus on the pushpin and have a partner take the shape stick and slide it slowly from one side of the semicircle to the center. With a pencil, mark where you first see the color of the shape, recognize the shape itself, and finally where you clearly have focused on the shape.

9. When you are done testing each of the four shapes, record your data in the table on the opposite page. Make one data table for each person that you test.

FOCAL PIN

RECOGNITION MARK

NOSE SLOT

Data & Observations

Color/Shape	First See	Recognize	Clear Focus
Blue /Square			
Red/ Triangle			
Yellow/ Octagon			
Green/Circle			

How Come, Huh?

The retina at the back of the eyeball has a bunch of light-sensitive cells we call cones and rods. Colors are sensed by the cones while black, white, and shades of grey are sensed by the rods. The cones and rods are most tightly packed in the middle of the retina, which is why things look sharpest right in front of where you are looking.

Your peripheral vision is created when light enters your field of view from the side. The cones and rods that are on the edges of the retina detect motion, color, and then shape. It may not be clear, but you know that the object is there.

Science Fair Extensions

13. Use your peripheral vision to draw a picture. It is difficult, but create the illustration without ever directly looking at the object you are drawing.

14. Assemble some paper "blinders" like the kind you see placed on horses sometimes, and spend some time without your peripheral vision. Explain how it affected your vision, why this could be a good thing if you are taking a skitterish horse into a busy area, and why it might not be so good if you were playing basketball.

15. Compare the peripheral vision of a group of athletes with that of a group of musicians, artists, or math junkies. See if the athletes have better peripheral vision than any of these other groups. Or is their peripheral vision the same or worse than people in these other groups?

Disappearing Frog

The Experiment

You can think of the optic nerve as the data cord that plugs into each eye and connects your brain to your peepers. The blind spot in each eye is the area where the optic nerve connects to the back of your eyeball. There are no receptors located there, so you do not perceive an image in that part of your field of view. But don't believe us, figure it out for yourself.

Materials

1 Book with Frog and •
1 Meter Stick
2 Eyes

Procedure

1. Photocopy the dot and frog on top of the next page. Cut out along the dotted line and place the card on a meter stick.

2. To find your blind spot, close your left eye and stare at the **frog** with your right eye. You should be able to see both the **dot** and the **frog**. Concentrate on the **frog** and *slowly* move the card toward your face. At some point the **dot** will disappear from your field of view. Hold the card in that position. The light reflected from the **dot** is now striking the blind spot at the back of your eyeball. Note the distance from your eye to the card and record that information in the data and observation section.

3. After you have found your blind spot, continue to move the card toward your face slowly and the **dot** will reappear. Move the card in and out, observing the image of the **dot**.

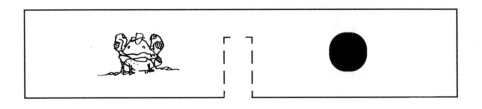

4. Repeat this experiment closing your right eye, staring at the **dot**, and looking for the **frog** to disappear. Close your right eye and stare at the **dot** with your left. Slowly move the card back and forth until the **frog** disappears from your view as you look at the **dot**. That is your blind spot. Note the distance from your eye to the book and record that information in the Data and Observation Section.

Data & Observations

Eye	Distance from eye to card (cm)
Left	
Right	

How Come, Huh?

Your blind spot is the area of your eye where the cable to your brain, the optic nerve, connects to the back of your eyeball. There are no light receptors located there, so you do not perceive an image in that part of your field of view when light strikes it.

Science Fair Extensions

16. Measure and record the distance for blind spots (for both eyes) in girls and boys, and determine if there is any difference between the sexes.

17. As we grow older lots of things change, including the shape of the eye. Create an experiment where you determine if there is a difference in the distance for the blind spot based on the age of the individual.

18. Determine if people with 20/20 vision, natural or laser-corrected, have a different blind spot measurement than people who need corrective lenses.

Visual Purple

The Experiment

The back of your eyeball gives residence to two different kinds of light-sensing receptors: rods and cones. The cones see color and the rods see black, white, and shades of gray. Our eyes adapt to darkness by producing a chemical called visual purple, which increases the ability of the rods to collect and transmit images in low-light situations. To increase the amount of light that enters the eyes, the diameter of the pupil (the black area in the middle of your iris) increases automatically. The increased amount of light and the production of visual purple makes it easier for us to see in darker places.

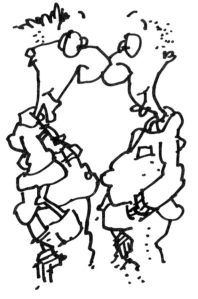

Materials

1   Dark Room
1   Light Switch
1   Lab Partner with Pupil Reflex
1   Pencil

Procedure

1. Darken the room and allow your eyes to acclimate to the dark for five minutes. Over the course of this experiment, as you read the text on this page, it should get noticeably easier each time you look at the page.

2. When your eyes have adjusted to the low light for a couple of minutes, draw a picture of your lab partner's eye in the left box in the data section.

3. Flip the lights on and observe what happens to the size of your partner's pupil as it is flooded with light.

4. Once the light is on, draw a second picture of what your lab partner's eye looks like, paying special attention to the pupil.

Data & Observations

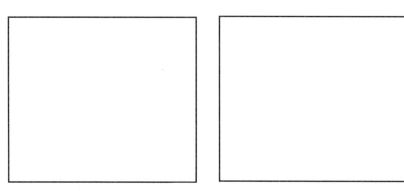

Lab partner's eye as seen in a dark room with little light

Lab partner's eye as seen in a light room with lots of light

How Come, Huh?

As the light enters the eye, the brain recognizes that there is a tremendous amount of light flooding the cones and rods. It doesn't like this, so it closes the size of the opening to restrict the amount of light. If you go outside on a bright sunny day after being in a dark house, you may notice that there is so much light that it actually hurts your eyes, and you have to squint and look down at the ground for a minute until your eyes adjust.

Science Fair Extensions

19. Photographers use a red light in the developing room. Experiment with measuring the size a pupil dilates and the speed that it recovers in red light versus a darkened room.

Holey Hands

The Experiment

Having two eyes gives us an opportunity to mix two different batches of information and see the same thing from two slightly different angles.

Materials

1 Sheet of Paper
1 Hand
2 Eyes

Procedure

1. Roll the piece of paper into a tube and hold it up to your right eye.

2. Keeping both eyes open place your open left hand in front of your left eye, (the eye that does not have the tube in front of it) about halfway down the tube. The illusion of a hole in the palm of your left hand should be created by your brain.

How Come, Huh?

This phenomena is called stereoscopic vision, or vision from two perspectives. The right eye is looking through the tube and is sending that image to the brain. The left is looking at the palm of a hand and sending that image to the brain at the same time. The brain decides to process both images at the same time and creates the illusion that you just saw, a hole in the palm of your hand.

Big Idea 4

White light is composed of all the colors of the rainbow: red, orange, yellow, green, blue, indigo, and violet. White light can be separated into all of these colors when it passes through a prism or diffraction grating.

© 2000 • B. K. Hixson

Prisms, Water Prisms

The Experiment

Water can act as a prism. Anyone who has seen a rainbow after a big rainstorm will tell you that for a fact. You are going to take advantage of the refractive characteristics (the ability to split white light into the colors of the rainbow) of water to create a rainbow using a tub of water, a mirror, and a flashlight.

Materials

1   2 to 5 Gallon Plastic Tub
1   Mirror, Large
1   Piece of Black Cardboard or Construction Paper
1   Pair of Scissors
1   Roll of Masking Tape
1   Flashlight
1   Sheet of White Construction Paper
1   Room, Dark
1   Prism
1   Box of Crayons

PAPER W/SLIT

TAPE

FLASHLIGHT

Procedure

1. Fill the plastic tub three-fourths full with water. Place the tub on the table and then lean the mirror against the far inside end wall of the tub.

2. Cut a horizontal slit in the black construction paper that is one-quarter of an inch tall and the width of the flashlight lens.

3. Tape the black construction square to the flashlight lens so the light shines through the slit.

4. Place the white construction paper on the table, place the prism on one of its ends, darken the room, and shine the slit of light into the prism. Experiment with where the light enters the prism until you see a bright colorful rainbow projected onto the sheet of paper. Record your observations on the next page in the spaces that have been provided.

5. This part of the lab requires a little practice. Holding the flashlight in one hand and the white construction paper in the other, shine the light through the water onto the mirror. This is the experimental part; move the white construction paper up and down until you find the beam of reflected light bouncing off the mirror and up through the water again. You will see a rainbow. Record your observations on the next page.

Prisms, Water Prisms

Data & Observations

Record your observations in the spaces below. Draw a picture of the rainbows that were produced by the two different experiments. Be sure to draw the colors in the order that you saw them.

Rainbow produced by glass prism   *Rainbow produced by water & mirror*

How Come, Huh?

1. In the first experiment, the white light containing all of the colors of the rainbow entered the glass prism. Once it hit the glass, the different wavelengths of light bent at different angles as they traveled through the glass. This separated them from one another. When they reemerged on the other side of the prism, you could see the individual colors.

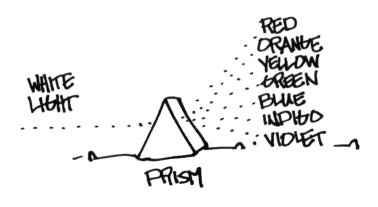

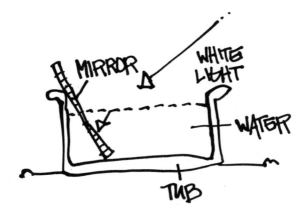

2. In the second half of the experiment the same thing happens. The flashlight beam is composed of all the colors of the rainbow mixed together. As long as they are traveling through air, they travel at the same speed, but when they hit the water they are bent at different angles and separate out. They are still traveling the same speed but in different lanes now. This produces the rainbow you see.

Science Fair Extensions

20. See if you can continue to separate the colors further by lining up a second prism in the rainbow of the first.

21. Figure out a way to gather up the colors that have been produced and mix them back together to produce white light again.

22. Experiment with moving the flashlight and paper closer to the mirror and farther away. Draw a picture and be able to predict what happens to the size and clarity of the rainbow image.

23. You can also create a rainbow on a sunny day using a garden hose with a fine-spray nozzle attached. Set the nozzle adjustment so that a fine mist is produced and move the mist around in the sunshine until you see the rainbow. This works better if the sun is lower in the sky; late afternoon is best.

Dissecting White Light

The Experiment

Dissection! Doesn't that word bring blood and guts to mind? If you were dissecting a once-living thing, this might be true, but you will be dissecting without a scalpel and forceps. Instead, you will be taking apart light with a plastic film that has thousands of tiny slits in it. Sounds more like a magic trick than dissection, but it works. Lab, please.

Materials

1 Pair of Diffraction Grating Glasses
3 Sources of White Light (NEVER USE THE SUN!)
    1 Fluorescent Bulb
    1 Incandescent Bulb
    1 Candle Flame
1 Commercial Spectroscope
1 Set of Colored Pencils

Procedure

1. Put on the diffraction glasses and take a look at the fluorescent lights that are in the room. You should see a complete set of the colors of the rainbow. Record them in the correct order, in the spaces on the next page, starting with red. Draw a picture of the rainbows as they appear around the light.

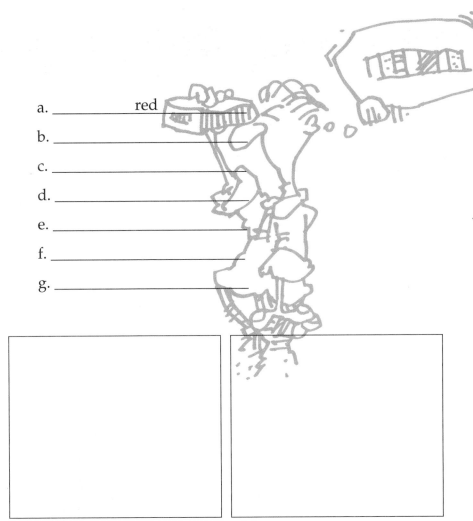

a. _____ red
b. _____
c. _____
d. _____
e. _____
f. _____
g. _____

Flourescent light thru diffraction grating   *Flourescent light thru a spectroscope*

2. Now observe the same light using the commercial spectroscope. Record your observations in the spaces provided.

3. Repeat steps 1 and 2 using the diffraction grating and the spectroscope to observe an incandescent bulb and then, with the supervision of an adult, a candle flame. Record your observations in the spaces provided on the next page.

Dissecting White Light

Incandescent light thru diffraction grating   *Incandescent light thru a spectroscope*

Candle light thru diffraction grating   *Candle light thru a spectroscope*

How Come, Huh?

Diffraction grating is a special plastic film material that does the equivalent of what a prism can do. It splits the light you are viewing into its spectra, or special color pattern, created by the elements that emit it. Different elements produce different and very unique color patterns that are seen when viewed through the spectroscope. These color patterns are unique to each element and can be used to identify the element much the same way that fingerprints can be used to identify people.

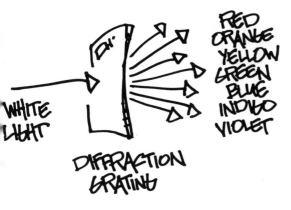

WHITE LIGHT

DIFFRACTION GRATING

RED
ORANGE
YELLOW
GREEN
BLUE
INDIGO
VIOLET

As light travels through the diffraction grating, the different wavelengths "bend" and separate into the same sequence as the colors of the rainbow. The difference in the wavelengths is what produces the different colors. The shorter ones are the blues and violets. The longer ones are the reds and oranges.

When you look through a spectroscope, you will find that the color print consists of separate lines rather than large, wide bands like you see when a rainbow appears after a storm. The number and location of the color bands— red, orange, yellow, green, blue, and so on— is unique and is only found with that one element or compound.

Science Fair Extensions

24. There are sealed tubes of gas that can be electrified to excite the electrons. When these tubes are plugged in and viewed through a spectroscope, they produce specific color patterns. Create a display where these tubes of gas can be viewed and compare to samples that have been burned in a flame.

25. Astronomers use finely tuned diffraction gratings to filter starlight that is collected through telescopes. This light can tell the astronomers what age the star is, its composition, and how fast it is moving away from the Earth. Collect information and build a spectrophotometer that can be used to view starlight.

26. Forensic labs that investigate crimes use spectroscopes to identify substances that are collected at the scene of the crime. Visit one of these labs and glean what information and technical data you can and use it to construct your own instrument.

Powdered-Milk Sunsets

The Experiment

And then there is the age-old question queried from youngster to parent, "Dad, why is the sky blue?" If you are in the majority, you will draw a blank until you get done with this lab. We'll also explain why sunsets are red, orange, and yellow but rarely green or violet.

Materials

1   Large Clear Container (Baking Dish)
    Water
1   Flashlight
1   Index card
1   Container of Powdered Milk
1   Spoon

Procedure

1. Fill the container with water and set it on a level surface.

2. Place the flashlight so that it shines through the container lengthwise and the beam can be reflected off a white index card.

3. Add powdered milk to the water a pinch at a time, stirring with the spoon, until you can see the beam as it shines through the liquid.

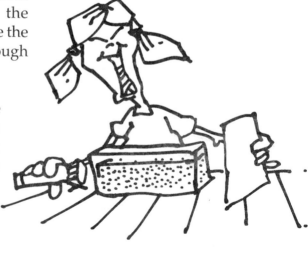

4. Look at the beam of light from the side of the container and at the end of the container. Record the colors that you see in the data table on the next page.

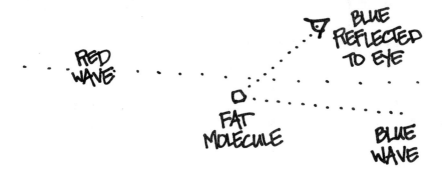

Data & Observations

Location	Color(s)
End	
Side	

How Come, Huh?

As the sunlight enters our atmosphere, it bounces off the gas molecules. The faster blue wavelengths of light tend to run into and be scattered by the gas molecules more. The longer red and orange wavelengths tend to zip on by and go directly to the Earth. The same thing happens in the milky water. The blue wavelengths tend to bounce into the fat molecules and get scattered sideways, whereas the red-orange waves cruise on through to the end of the tank.

Science Fair Extensions

27. Experiment with the powder you add. Try cornstarch, talcum powder, chalk dust, and so forth.

28. Scattered light becomes polarized. Grab a polarizing filter and look at the end of the tank and rotate the filter to notice the variance in the intensity of light.

Roy Boy's Wind Sock

The Experiment

Creating this rainbow wind sock will help you learn and remember the colors of the rainbow. It will also let you see that wave frequency, defined as the number of waves that pass by a point each second, is different for every color. Red light has the longest waves so it takes them more time to parade on by. This means that red has a low frequency. Violet light, on the other hand, is a short, squatty wave that zips right along. Because lots of waves pass by a point, it is said to have a high frequency. All of the other colors fall somewhere in between.

Materials

1   Sheet of White Paper
1   Hole Punch
1   Pair of Scissors
1   Bottle of White Glue
7   Strips of Curling Ribbon
    (one of each rainbow color)
1   Meter of White Yarn

Procedure

1. Cut a strip of white paper (45 cm x 10 cm) to make a cylinder.On the top edge of the paper, mark holes at 15 cm, 30 cm, and 45 cm. Along the bottom edge mark holes at 6 cm, 12 cm, 18 cm, 24 cm, 30 cm, 36 cm, and 42 cm. Glue the ends together.

2. Using the marks you have made, punch three holes evenly around the top of the paper and seven holes evenly around the bottom.

3. This is where you get to use your imagination a bit. Take the seven rainbow strips of ribbon that represent the different wavelengths of visible light and cut them to different lengths proportional to their actual wavelengths. The tricky part will be to remember that you are only measuring one wavelength, which is different than the very first exercise in this book where we took a standard length, 1 centimeter, and stretched out all the waves that were present in that distance.

4. Thread each of the strips of ribbon through the holes that you have marked and punched, and tie them off. Add them to the cylinder in the same order you would find them in the rainbow.

5. Finally, add white yarn to the 3 holes on the top to hang your design by. Display it from the ceiling of your room. The white strip and white yarn represent all the colors combined to make white light.

Data & Observations

In the space below, list the colors of the rainbow in order beginning with red. If you need help, read forward and find out what Roy G. Biv stands for.

Colors	Length of ribbon (cm)
_____	_____
_____	_____
_____	_____
_____	_____
_____	_____
_____	_____
_____	_____

Roy Boy's Wind Sock

How Come, Huh?

The color of light depends upon the frequency. Frequency is the number of waves that pass by a point each second. Red, orange, yellow, green, blue, indigo, and violet light waves have different frequencies; however, when combined they make up white light. Thus we have Roy G. Biv.

Violet light on the electromagnetic spectrum has a high frequency and a short wavelength while red light has a longer wavelength and a lower frequency. The length of the ribbon may be cut to represent the wavelengths of the colors. Red would be the longest, violet the shortest and the others in between.

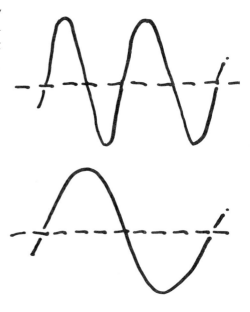

Science Fair Extensions

29. Expand your display to include the entire electromagnetic spectrum from radio and television waves to X rays and gamma rays. You may want to use colored ribbon or yarn for the visible light spectrum, and after that your creativity and imagination get to run wild. You could cut up old hospital X rays or paste together sections of the TV guide. Have fun. This is more of a report than a science fair project.

30. Create a display of the instruments that collect the different wavelengths. Explain when they were invented and by whom, how they work, and any other significant events that transpired.

Big Idea 5

Red, blue, and yellow are the primary colors of the rainbow. These three colors can be mixed in a variety of combinations and produce all of the other colors that we see.

Mixing Color Tubes

The Experiment

Red, yellow, and blue are the three primary colors. From these three colors all of the other colors of the rainbow and paint card can be mixed. This lab will allow you to mix the basic colors together and produce secondary colors.

Materials

- 3 Large, Pre-form Tubes
- 3 Test Tube Caps
-   Water
- 1 Bottle of Red Food Coloring
- 1 Bottle of Blue Food Coloring
- 1 Bottle of Yellow Food Coloring
- 1 Light Source
- 1 Box of Crayons

FOOD COLORING

+

WATER

↓

PRE-FORM TUBE

Procedure

1. Fill the pre-form tubes three-fourths full with water. Add several drops of red food coloring to the first tube, cap, and shake vigorously.

2. Repeat the procedure in the other tubes with yellow and blue food-coloring dyes.

3. Using the illustration to the right as a guide, hold the red and yellow tubes up to the light and observe what color is produced where the two tubes cross. Record that color in the data section.

4. Repeat the procedure mixing red and blue, and then blue and yellow.

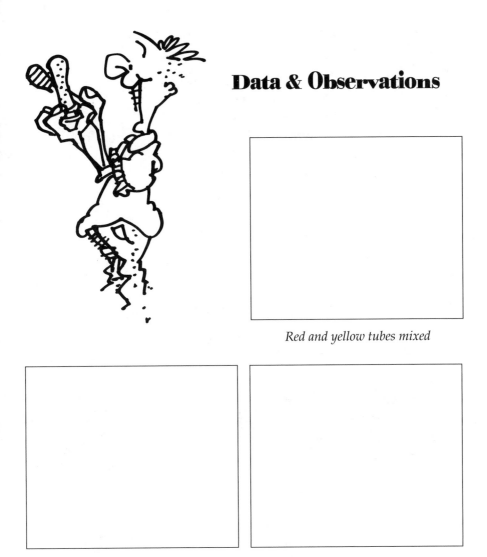

Data & Observations

Red and yellow tubes mixed

Red and blue tubes mixed

Blue and yellow tubes mixed

How Come, Huh?

As the light travels through the tubes, the wavelengths produced by the food coloring mix together and average one another out to produce the secondary colors that you see.

Jerry Garcia's Milk Shake

The Experiment

We are going to take advantage of a change in environment, specifically the pH of a solution, to create a variety of colors from the three primary colors. Whole milk contains fats and proteins that are very sensitive to changes in pH. If the pH is raised or lowered, even just a bit, it causes these long molecules to bend, wiggle, and fold around one another. This mixes the food coloring you added to the milk and produces a Jerry Garcia Milk Shake.

Materials

1   9"-12" Pie Tin
1   Pint of Whole Milk, Warm
1   Bottle of Red Food Coloring
1   Bottle of Blue Food Coloring
1   Bottle of Yellow Food Coloring
1   Bottle of Liquid Soap
1   Box of Crayons

Procedure

1. Fill the pie tin with warm, whole milk. Cream or half-and-half also works very well.

2. Using the three primary colors of food coloring, create a small equilateral triangle, 1" on a side, in the center of the milk. Using two drops of each food color works well. Use the illustration on the next page as a guide.

Observe the movement of the food coloring for about 60 seconds.

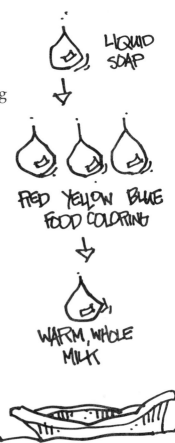

LIQUID SOAP

RED   YELLOW   BLUE
FOOD COLORING

WARM, WHOLE MILK

PIE TIN

RED

SOAP

BLUE   YELLOW

3. Add a drop of liquid soap to the very center of the triangle. You should immediately notice the effect the soap has on the proteins and fats in the milk.

Once the reaction starts to slow down, add drops of soap to different areas around the pie tin and the reaction will start up again.

How Come, Huh?

Protein and fat molecules are very long and complex. They have several kinds of bonds, or connections, holding them together. When you added the liquid soap, you raised the pH of the milk and the soap started stealing the hydrogen atoms from these long molecules. This caused the proteins and fats to collapse and curl up into large clumps. Consequently, this collapsing bumped the food-coloring molecules and mixed them with one another.

Science Fair Extensions

31. Repeat the experiment and use a variety of different milks: nonfat, 1 percent, 2 percent, whole, and cream. Keep the temperature the same and record the difference in the way the colors are produced.

32. Repeat the experiment but change the temperature of the milk and see if that has any effect on the rate the colors are mixed.

33. Repeat the reaction with other bases (ammonia, bleach, etc.) and acids (lemon juice, vinegar). Determine if pH is a factor based on your observations.

Rainbow in a Bag

The Experiment

This is a fun activity much like the previous one where you get to make all sorts of different colors by mixing the three primary colors together and then mixing the secondary and tertiary colors with one another.

Materials

1   Box of Cornstarch
    Water
1   1 Quart Saucepan
1   Spoon
1   Ziplock Baggie
1   Bottle of Red Food Coloring
1   Bottle of Blue Food Coloring
1   Bottle of Yellow Food Coloring
1   Box of Crayons

Procedure

1. Add one-quarter of the box of cornstarch to the saucepan. Slowly add water to the cornstarch and stir with the spoon. Continue to add water and stir with the spoon until you produce a thick, sticky mixture that resembles custard.

2. Pour all of the cornstarch goo into the baggie. Add a drop of red, blue, and yellow food coloring to each side and the middle of the goo and seal the baggie.

3. Knead the baggie and observe the colors that are produced.

Data & Observations

Continue to squish the baggie, mixing the three primary colors until you have produced at least 12 different colors. Find crayons that match as closely as possible. Color the circles below.

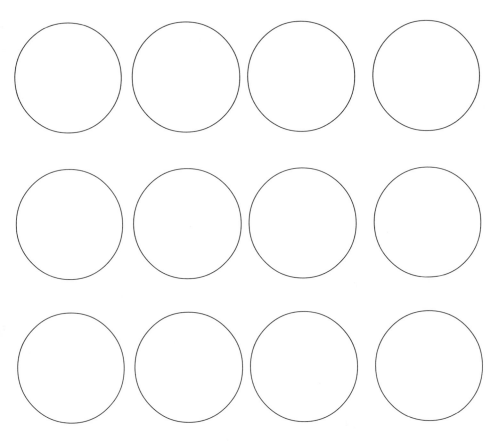

How Come, Huh?

The food color mixes with and sticks to the cornstarch concoction that you made. As you mix the colors, they blend with one another, producing new colors. Depending on the percentage of pigment, you should get all of the colors of the rainbow and more.

Big Idea 6

When light strikes an object, it can be completely reflected or it can be absorbed, diffused, or transmitted. The terms used to describe these phenomenon are *opaque*, *translucent*, and *transparent*.

The Shadow Knows

The Experiment

As light travels it encounters a variety of objects. If the object absorbs or reflects all of the light, it is said to be *opaque*. Shadows are created when light is blocked by an opaque object.

In this lab we are going to experiment with light and its ability to "bend" or "curve" around straight edges.

Materials

1 Sheet of Black Construction Paper
1 Pair of Scissors
1 Roll of Masking Tape
1 Craft Stick
1 Meter Stick
1 Light Source
1 Darkened Room

Procedure

1. Cut a pattern out of the black construction paper and tape it to the top of the craft stick. It can be as simple as a square or triangle or as complex as the shape of an animal like a rhinoceros or dinosaur. You choose.

2. Place the end of the meter stick against a clear spot on the wall and hold the craft stick at the 1 centimeter mark. Place the light source at the twenty centimeter mark, and then draw what you see on the next page.

3. Move the craft stick to 10 centimeters and keep the light source at 20 centimeters. Record your observations.

4. Move the craft stick to 19 centimeters and keep the light source at 20 centimeters. Record your observations.

The Shadow Knows

5. Place the meter stick against a clear spot on the wall and hold the craft stick at the 1 centimeter mark. Place the light source at the 5 centimeter mark and draw what you see on the next page.

6. Repeat the experiment keeping the craft stick at 1 cm and moving the light source back to 10 centimeters, and then 15 centimeters. Record your observations in the space on the next page.

Data & Observations

Craft stick @ 1 cm, light source @ 20cm   *Craft stick @ 10 cm, light source @ 20cm*

Craft stick @ 19 cm, light source @ 20cm

Craft stick @ 1 cm, light source @ 5cm   *Craft stick @ 1 cm, light source @ 10cm*

Craft stick @ 1 cm, light source @ 15 cm

How Come, Huh?

This is one of the great mysteries that has yet to be solved. "Does light travel in a straight line, or does it curve?" Some experiments suggest one thing and other experiments suggest another.

This experiment supports the curved idea. If light truly traveled in a straight line, then the shadow cast by the image would always be sharp and clear. But, as you see in this experiment, the closer the image gets to the light source the fuzzier its shadow becomes. The light appears to curve around the edges of the image and produce an indistinct line. Figure it out and the Nobel Prize is yours for the taking.

T. P. Binoculars

The Experiment

When light strikes an object, it can be completely reflected, absorbed, diffused, or transmitted. The terms used to describe these phenomena are *opaque, translucent,* and *transparent.* They are the focus of this lab.

You will do two things for this lab. First you will make binoculars using toilet paper tubes. Second, you will go on a scavenger hunt and locate objects around your house that are opaque, translucent, and transparent.

Materials

1   Sheet of Wax Paper
1   Sheet of Aluminum Foil
1   Sheet of Clear Plastic Wrap
1   Pair of Scissors
2   Rubber Bands
2   Toilet Paper Tubes

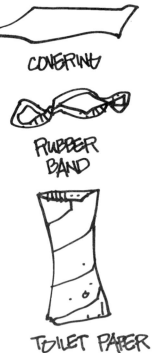

COVERING

RUBBER BAND

Procedure

1. Cut each of the sheets of wax paper, aluminum foil, and clear plastic wrap in half.

2. Take one of the sheets of aluminum foil and wrap it around the end of one of the toilet paper tubes. Secure it with one of the rubber bands. Do the same thing with the other toilet paper tube and piece of aluminum foil, so that you have a matched set.

TOILET PAPER TUBE

3. Hold the tubes up to your eyes and attempt to walk around the room. Record your observations in the data table on the next page.

4. Repeat the procedure making and using a set of wax paper binoculars, and clear plastic wrap binoculars. Record your observations in the data table below.

5. Finally, go on a scavenger hunt around your house and find items that are opaque, transparent, and translucent. List those items in the data table on the next page. Try to fill in the entire section.

Data & Observations

1. As you record your observations for this data table you will want to rate your "Ability to See" as: Excellent, Marginal, or Poor. You will also want to choose the "Vocabulary" word that best describes the binocular material. Your choices are *opaque, transparent,* and *translucent.* After you have completed the first three search your house and find other materials to try out on the binoculars.

Binocular Material	Ability to See	Vocabulary
Aluminum Foil		
Wax Paper		
Plastic Wrap		
1.		
2.		
3.		
4.		
5.		
6.		

T. P. Binoculars

2. Go on a light scavenger hunt around your house and "collect" as many items as you can for each word.

	Opaque	Transparent	Translucent
1.			
2.			
3.			
4.			
5.			
6.			
7.			
8.			
9.			
10.			

How Come, Huh?

The aluminum foil reflects all of the light that strikes it, so it is said to be *opaque*. The wax paper reflects some of the light that strikes it and allows some of it to pass through. This produces a fuzzy image that is described as *translucent*. Finally, the clear plastic allows virtually all of the light to pass through and is classified as *transparent*.

Science Fair Extensions

34. Do research on bats, cave salamanders, and insects in general to learn about the different vision abilities of these different kinds of animals. Use your understanding of how animals see to build models of how each different type of eye perceives the world.

35. Cataracts form in the eyes of some older people. This is now fortunately correctable with outpatient surgery. Find three to five people who have had cataracts and work with them to create a model of what their vision was like before the surgery.

Big Idea 7

Light emitted from different materials can be filtered and observed through a diffraction grating to produce characteristic patterns that are unique to that material. These patterns, or fingerprints, of light can be used to identify different kinds of materials.

Chemical Fingerprints

The Experiment

This activity will allow you to see the "fingerprints" from a variety of light sources. Not all light is the same. The light we see from a streetlight may be different than the light emitted by a flashlight or kerosene lantern. Spectroscopes have a special film called diffraction grating that acts like a prism to separate light into its colors. Different elements combine to make different light sources. These different combinations of elements make a pattern of color, called line spectra, that are unique to that light source. By using diffraction grating, you will learn about identifying different light sources by their "fingerprints."

Materials

1   Propane Torch
1   Nichrome Wire
1   Bottle of 10% Hydrochloric Acid
1   Bottle of Strontium Chloride Solution
1   Commercial Spectroscope
1   Bottle of Potassium Chloride Solution
1   Bottle of Barium Chloride Solution

Procedure

1. With the assistance and supervision of an adult light a propane torch. If you have not reviewed fire safety procedures, now is a good time.

2. Dip the nichrome wire in the diluted hydrochloric acid. While it is wet, dip the wire in the strontium chloride and then place the wire in the flame of the torch. Observe the color that is produced and record it in the data on the next page.

3. Now darken the room and repeat the procedure of burning the strontium in the flame, only this time look at the colors through the spectroscope. The diffraction grating will produce thin lines of different colors. Try your very best to determine how many lines of each color are produced and where they are located. Record your observations in the data table below.

4. Repeat the procedure for the other two chemicals and record your observations below.

Data & Observations

Chemical Tested	Flame Test Colors Seen	
	Naked Eye	Through Spectroscope
Strontium Chloride		
Potassium Chloride		
Barium Chloride		

Chemical Fingerprints

Data & Observations

Draw a picture of the color bands that you saw through the spectroscope.

Chemicals	Colors Seen Through Spectroscope
Strontium Chloride	
Potassium Chloride	
Barium Chloride	

How Come, Huh?

Astronomers use the light received through spectroscopes to learn about objects in space. This light carries information about the stars' temperature, composition, magnetic fields, and motion. This information is decoded by splitting the light into a spectrum using a spectroscope. The bright line spectrum that results is often called an emission spectrum or a characteristic spectrum. Every atom has an individual and characteristic spectrum, much like every person has a fingerprint, which can be used for the identification because it is like no one else's.

Science Fair Extensions

36. Some of the science supply companies carry tubes full of gases that can be excited (meaning that they glow) using an electric current. When these tubes are plugged in, you can view them through a spectroscope and see the characteristic bands that are produced by specific chemicals. Mix and view combinations of the tubes to show how these fingerprints can be used in identifying substances.

37. Test some common elements and identify their color band fingerprints. Ask a friend to mix various combinations of these chemicals and see if you can correctly identify the mixture they have put together.

Homemade 'Scope

The Experiment

As we saw in the previous experiment, a spectroscope is an instrument that collects a small sample of light at one end and then splits that sample with a piece of diffraction grating at the other end. As the light sample passes through the diffraction grating, it separates into specific bands of light. This sequence is unique to every element and compound, and it provides a fingerprint of that element that can later be used to identify mystery compounds.

In this experiment you are going to make your own spectroscope using a toilet paper tube, aluminum foil, and diffraction grating.

Materials

1   Toilet Paper Tube
1   Rubber Band
1   4" by 4" piece of Aluminum Foil
1   Pair of Scissors
1   Penknife or Dissecting Scalpel
1   Piece of Diffraction Grating.
1   Source of Light

Procedure

1. Take the toilet paper tube and cut a narrow slot on one end. The slot should go almost all the way through the tube.

2. Place the aluminum foil over the end opposite the cut in the tube and fix it in place with the rubber band. Make a narrow slit in the aluminum foil with the knife or dissecting scalpel.

© 2000 • B. K. Hixson

Homemade 'Scope

3. Slide the diffraction grating into the slot that you created in step one.

4. Turn the flashlight on and shine the light toward the slit in the aluminum foil. Look at the back of the diffraction grating and see if a pattern is produced.

There are a couple of things you can do if you do not see specific bands of light. One, make sure the slit in the aluminum foil is either perfectly vertical or horizontal to the diffraction grating. Also, taking the diffraction grating out and rotating it 90° sometimes helps. This is science; sometimes you are going to have to tweak your equipment a little bit before it performs the way you want it to.

How Come, Huh?

As the light strikes the slit at the end of the tube, only a small amount makes it to the diffraction grating. This sliver of light is then sorted by the color lines in the grating producing the line spectra.

Science Fair Extensions

38. Once you get the hang of it, design several other kinds of spectroscopes and build them. Rate their performance, figure out their weaknesses, and show a history of development for each one.

Big Idea 8

White light can be polarized using a special filter that allows certain wavelengths of light to pass through while blocking others.

Light Blocker

The Experiment

Polarized sunglasses are used to explore the vibrating patterns of visible light. Snow skiers, fishermen, and boaters use polarized sunglasses to reduce light glare bouncing off snow and water. In this experiment one lens is placed in front of a beam of light and then a second lens is added. The lenses are then rotated to allow more or less light to pass through.

Materials

2   Polarizing Filters
1   Flashlight
1   Sheet of Black Paper
1   White Crayon

Procedure

1. Turn on the flashlight and observe the brightness of the beam on a sheet of black paper. Record your observations in the data section on the next page, using the white crayon.

2. Place one polarized lens in front of the light source and observe the change in brightness you see. Use the illustration on the top of the next page as a guide. Again, record your observations in the data section on the next page.

3. Place the second polarized lens in front of the first lens and compare the brightness again. Record your observations in the data section on the next page using that same white crayon.

4. Finally, rotate the second lens 90 degrees, keeping it in front of the first lens, and observe the brightness of the beam of light as the wavelengths are filtered out.

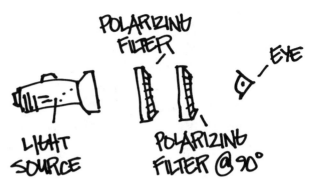

Data & Observations

1. Unfiltered flashlight beam

2. Filtered with one polarizing filter

3. Filtered with two polarizing filters

4. One polarizing filter at 90 degrees

Light Blocker

How Come, Huh?

Visible light moves in transverse waves that have crests and troughs. Some vibrate vertically, some horizontally, and others at various angles. *Polarized lenses allow only light waves vibrating in a vertical plane to pass through. All of the others are reflected,* as in the illustration below. This reduces the light in brightness and does away with glare. As the second lens is rotated, it changes the orientation of its horizontal plane and begins blocking the passage of some light waves that made it through the first lens. When the planes of the two lens are perpendicular, all light waves are blocked.

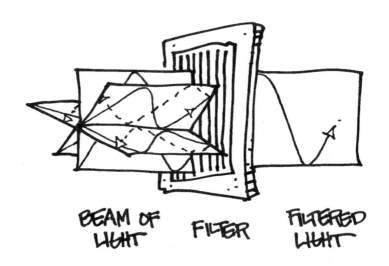

BEAM OF LIGHT   FILTER   FILTERED LIGHT

Science Fair Extensions

39. Repeat this experiment and vary the light source. Use fluorescent light, incandescent light, natural (sun) light, and a laser. Show the differences, if any, by drawing the light images that you see on black construction paper.

40. Many sunglasses not only boast polarizing lenses but also the ability to block ultraviolet (UV) light as well. Look at the experiment on page 160 that uses beads that change color when they are exposed to ultraviolet light. Test the ability of different brands of sunglasses to block UV light and rate them.

Finding Stress Fractures

The Experiment

Growing, active students sometimes suffer stress fractures in their bones. This experiment with common plastics and polarized light filters will help you visualize a stress fracture and also understand light. CD or cassette cases and transparent plastic forks make good stress subjects. The case can be dismantled and stressed on different planes, vertically or horizontally, for each piece. The tines on the plastic forks can be stressed by compressing or separating them.

Materials

1   CD or Cassette Tape Case
1   Plastic Transparent Fork
    Assorted other Clear, Plastic, Pieces
1   Overhead Projector or Light Table
2   Pieces of Polarized Filter Paper

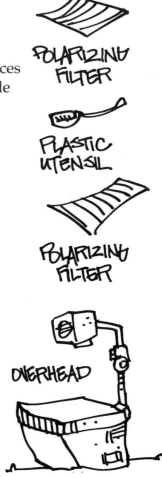

POLARIZING FILTER

PLASTIC UTENSIL

POLARIZING FILTER

Procedure

1. Arrange the overhead projector so that it shines on a screen or white wall surface. Place one piece of polarized filter paper on the overhead stage and put a fork on top of the filter. Draw what you see.

2. Take the fork and bend and distort the plastic piece. This will produce stress lines in the plastic.

3. Replace the fork on the overhead stage on top of the polarized paper and observe the stress lines that have been created.

OVERHEAD

Finding Stress Fractures

4. Place the second piece of polarized paper over the fork and observe the patterns. Record your observations in the space below.

5. Experiment with a number of different objects all made of transparent plastic. Finally, rotate the top piece of polarized paper ninety degrees so that it is exactly perpendicular to the original sheet.

Data & Observations

Plastic fork before it is stressed

Plastic fork after it is stressed

CD case before it is stressed

CD case after it is stressed

How Come, Huh?

White light vibrates as transverse waves in random directions. Polarized light is limited to waves vibrating in one plane by invisible lines in the polarized filter paper. To undersand this better think of light passing through the spaces in a picket fence, only waves vibrating vertically could slip through the spaces between fence pickets. All other angles of vibration would be blocked. Plastic refracts white light into colors in perpendicular polarized light waves. Each color produces a different pattern. The direction of the polarized color waves determines which ones will pass through the openings in the second polarized filter paper. When the plastic is bent to produce stress points, this alters the speed with which light travels through the plastic. Areas where colors change rapidly show high stress and areas where colors change slowly indicate low stress.

Remember, light travels in transverse waves. White light is made of the primary light colors: red, blue, and yellow. Forces applied to solids can produce stress fractures in the material.

Science Fair Extensions

41. Use red-, blue-, and yellow-colored cellophane paper on the overhead to demonstrate that you can produce white light by remixing the individual color wavelengths.

42. *Consumer Reports* time. Test the ability of different brands of plastic utensils to absorb and withstand stress. In other words, use the experiment to figure out which is the most durable plastic ware on the market. You can extend this idea to plastic plates, cups, containers, cases, and anything else plastic that you can find.

43. Use the principles of this experiment to test different materials such as glass, acrylic, polypropylene, acetate, and so on. See if the polarizing filters and light reflect stresses applied to these materials as well or if they are only good for plastics and, if so, possibly only certain kinds of plastics. Ralph Nader is watching so do a good job.

Hidden Mosaics

The Experiment

Transparent tape with a shiny, non-matte surface can be used to create colorful, abstract designs when it is applied to a piece of glass plate or a piece of Plexiglas™ and viewed through polarizing filters. You will make and view one of these designs.

Materials

1 Glass Plate
   or
1 Piece of Plexiglas™
1 Roll of Transparent Tape
2 Polarizing Filters
1 Source of Light

POLARIZING FILTER

GLASS WITH TAPE

POLARIZING FILTER

Procedure

1. Before you buy a pile of tape, take two polarizing filters into the office supply store and test a couple of brands to find the one that works best.

Place a small piece of the tape on one of the filters and rotate the other filter over it. If the tape turns from dark to light, it will work. If is stays the same intensity, you need to keep exploring.

2. When you find tape that will work, make a design by arranging strips on a glass plate in a random fashion. Make sure that several pieces crisscross and overlap.

LIGHT SOURCE

3. Place the finished plate between two polarizing filters and put everything on an overhead or up to a window on a bright, sunny day. Rotate the top piece of filter paper.

How Come, Huh?

1. For starters, the white light hits the first polarizing filter so only vertical wavelengths of all colors pass through.

2. That polarized light then zips on up into the tape. When each individual color hits the tape, it travels at a different speed (called the index of refraction), causing it to bend or rotate slightly. In other words, the tape acts sort of like a prism, sorting the white, polarized light into the colors of the rainbow. If the light passes through two or three pieces of tape stuck on top of one another, the light gets bent even more.

3. Then the light goes through the second polarizing filter, which transmits the light at different angles. As you rotate the top polarizing filter, you change the angle and the resulting color.

Science Fair Extensions

44. Experiment with different materials between the filters. Try plastic food containers, CD cases, plastic forks, drinking glasses. Determine why some materials work and others don't.

45. If you want to turn this into an art project, you can also cut the tape and produce letters. Tape your name, a picture of your house or favorite animal, and polarize them.

Polarized Sugar Water

The Experiment

White light contains all of the colors of the rainbow. When you polarize the light and allow it to pass through a sugar solution, you will be able to observe the changes in individual colors if you view the light through a second, rotating, polarizing filter or change the depth of the sugar solution. Cool, huh?

Materials

1   Large Cylinder, 3" in diameter
1   Small Cylinder, 2" in diameter
1   Bottle of Karo™ syrup
2   Polarizing Lenses
1   Bright Light

Procedure

1. Fill the large cylinder with a couple of inches of Karo™ syrup.

2. Put one polarizing filter under the base of the cylinder with the syrup.

3. Place the second, smaller cylinder into the syrup and place the second polarizing filter on top of that cylinder.

4. You should now have the setup pictured to the right. A small cylinder inside a large cylinder full of syrup. Polarizing filters on top and bottom and a very bright light shining up through the whole contraption.

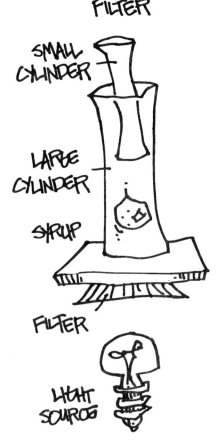

FILTER

SMALL CYLINDER

LARGE CYLINDER

SYRUP

FILTER

LIGHT SOURCE

5. Look down through the tube to the light source. Rotate the top polarizing filter slowly and look for color changes.

6. Now hold the filter still but change the depth of the syrup by moving the smaller tube up and down in the solution. Note the color changes that appear.

How Come, Huh?

As in the previous experiment, when polarized light enters the syrup it refracts, or rotates. The amount depends on the depth of the syrup. It also depends on the concentration of the syrup: The more concentrated the syrup is, the more the light is rotated. Finally, the amount of rotation is also keyed to the color. Blue waves, which are short, rotate more than red wavelengths, which are long.

So the light passes through the polarizing filter and into the syrup. There it strikes optically active molecules, which refract the white light into colors, like a prism. This light then travels through a second polarizing filter, which only allows certain wavelengths of color to pass through to our eyes. As the depth of the Karo™ sugar solution or the rotation of the second filter changes, the color also changes.

Science Fair Extensions

46. Rotate the filter and change the depth and see if you can keep the color constant.

47. Experiment with different types of syrup and see if there is a noticeable difference. Figure out what the heck "optically active" means and how it applies to this lab.

48. It has also been suggested that the concentration of the syrup affects the colors we see. Try a variety of dilutions to see if this is the case.

Big Idea 9

A lens is a tool that is used to bend, diffuse, magnify, or concentrate light. It can be made of glass, plastic, water, and other transparent kinds of materials.

Spoon Illusions

The Experiment
We know that light reflects off of smooth shiny surfaces. In that case, most spoons apply. The interesting thing about the reflection coming off a spoon is that it is right side up on one surface and upside down on another. Your job is to figure out which side of the spoon is like a convex lens and which side is like a concave lens and why.

Materials
1   Spoon with Good Reflection
1   Metric Ruler
1   Drawing Pencil
2   Sheets of Aluminum Foil
1   Empty 2-Liter Pop Bottle
1   Pair of Scissors
1   Roll of Tape

Procedure
1. Hold the spoon in your hand so the curved bottom portion is pointing toward you. Look at the image, which hopefully is you, and draw a picture of what you see as you hold the spoon 5 centimeters from your face.

2. Move the spoon to 30 centimeters from your face and draw a picture of what you see this time. Be as accurate as you can when you draw.

3. Flip the spoon over and look at the portion of the spoon that holds the soup when you eat. Draw a picture of the image you see as you hold the spoon 5 centimeters from your face.

4. Move the spoon to 30 centimeters from your face and draw a picture of what you see this time. Be as accurate as you can.

Spoon Illusions

Data & Observations

1. Draw the images you saw reflected in the spoon based on the position of the spoon and the distance it was from your face. Be as accurate as possible.

Image seen on bottom of spoon at 5 cm	*Image seen on bottom of spoon at 30 cm*
Image seen on inside of spoon at 5 cm	*Image seen on inside of spoon at 30 cm*

2. Cut the top and the bottom off a 2-liter pop bottle and then cut the remaining cylinder in half lengthwise. Smooth and tape a piece of aluminum foil to the inside of one half of the cylinder and smooth and tape another piece of aluminum foil to the outside of the other half. Repeat your spoon experiments with the aluminum foil coated cylinders.

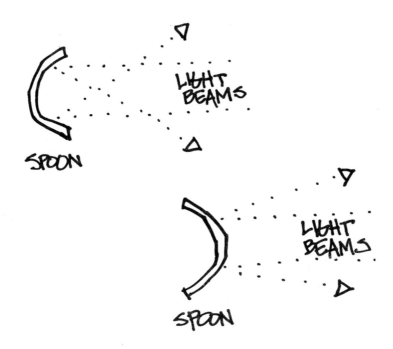

How Come, Huh?

When you are looking at the bottom of the spoon and the outside of the coated 2-liter pop bottle, you are actually looking at a convex lens. See bottom illustration above. The light image striking the surface is bent outward and away from the surface. This produces an image that looks larger and larger the farther you are from the reflective surface.

When you flip the spoon over or look on the inside of the coated 2-liter pop bottle, you have a concave lens. See top illustration. The light strikes the surface and is immediately reflected and crossed, flipping the image you see upside down. Depending on where you are from the reflected surface, the image is either right side up or upside down.

Science Fair Extensions

49. Collect a wide variety of spoons and other "curved" surfaces and compare the image that is reflected.

50. Compare actual concave and convex lenses with the lenses you create.

Portable Lenses

The Experiment

Understanding the shape of a lens and how it will change an image to our eyes also helps to explain some of the properties of light. You will be able to compare a magnifying glass lens in this activity to a water lens and learn about refracting light. You might want to assemble a variety of curved mirrors and lenses for further study. The mirrors that are sometimes used for putting on makeup, that magnify your skin so your pores could be mapped by the Geologic Survey folks, are great.

Materials

1   Washer, 3/8" Inside Diameter
1   Microscope Slide
1   Container of Petroleum Jelly
1   Piece of Newsprint with Lots of Type
1   Pipette, 1 mL
    Water

Procedure

1. Carefully smear a small amount of petroleum jelly on the flat side of the washer. There are two different sides, rounded and flat. Be sure to smear the flat side.

2. Place the washer on the center of the microscope slide with the jelly side down. Give it a half a twist to "seat" the washer. This makes a watertight seal so water doesn't sneak away unknowingly.

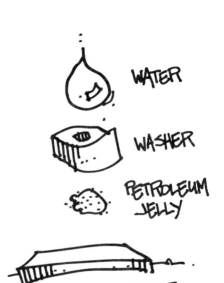

WATER

WASHER

PETROLEUM JELLY

SLIDE

3. Place the washer/slide combo on a piece of newspaper that has a lot of print. Take the pipette and fill it with water and slowly fill the inside of the washer with water until it is "domed" up.

4. Select the letter *e* from the text, place the lens over it, and draw a picture of what it looks like viewed through the convex lens that you have just constructed. Draw your observations in the space provided below.

5. Using the pipette, remove water from inside the washer until you have created a dip, similar to the cartoon pictured on the next page. Place the lens over the same letter *e* from the text and draw a picture of what it looks like viewed through the concave lens that you have just constructed. Draw your observations in the space provided below.

Data & Observations

e *viewed through concave lens*   e *viewed through convex lens*

Portable Lenses

How Come, Huh?

Lenses make for cool exploration, but how do they work? A convex lens bows outward away from the center. It can be this way on one side or both sides of the lens. In this activity, the water lens has one flat side against the slide and a side that is domed up toward the ceiling. As the light comes up from the bottom and out of the curved outer surface, the waves of light are spread apart, or refracted, so the image appears larger.

When you have a concave lens, or one that dips inward toward the center of the lens, the opposite is true. The light waves are brought closer together making the image appear smaller. The illustrations should help.

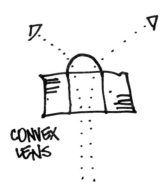

A convex lens bends the light image outward, expanding the appearance of the image you see.

Science Fair Extensions

51. Try to make a "Fun House" mirror that makes you look tall or squatty. The best way to approach this task is to acquire a sheet of polished metal or aluminum foil. Check with a sign company or your mom's kitchen drawer.

52. Collect a variety of shiny or see-through materials, and compare how they can distort an image. Classify each item as a concave or convex lens.

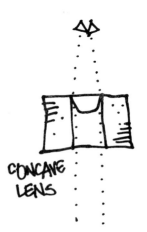

53. Visit the local opthomalogist for an office tour and a complete and total disruption of their business day and ability to earn an income.

A concave lens bends the light image inward, reducing the appearance of the image you see.

Cardboard Lenses

The Experiment

Lenses are fun to experiment with. In this activity, you will come to understand how a convex lens is shaped and how it is able to concentrate light. You will also experience the ability to magnify with it. It is an extension of the previous activity.

Materials

1   Piece of Cardboard, 10-15 square cm
1   Quarter
1   Plastic Wrap, 15-20 square cm
1   Pair of scissors
1   Roll of Masking Tape
1   1 mL Plastic Pipette
    Water
1   Sheet of Newspaper
1   Ruler

Procedure

1. Locate the middle of your cardboard square. Trace the quarter and cut a hole in the cardboard.

2. Cut a piece of plastic wrap that fits over the hole. Lay it over the hole and allow it to sag down into the hole just a bit. Make sure it overlaps enough so that you can use the masking tape to secure its edges to the cardboard and hold it in place.

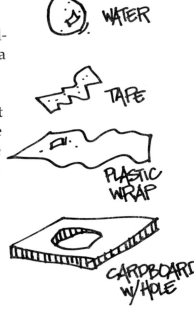

PIPETTE

WATER

TAPE

PLASTIC WRAP

CARDBOARD w/ HOLE

Cardboard Lenses

3. Using your pipette, make a puddle of water in the center of the plastic wrap. It should stay within the "boundaries" of the hole in the cardboard and produce a slight bulge. This is a convex lens.

4. Select the letter *e* from the newspaper text, place the lens over it and draw a picture of what it looks like viewed through the convex lens you have just constructed. Draw your observations in the space provided below.

5. Using the pipette, remove water from inside the plastic until you have created a dip. Place this new lens over the same letter *e* from the text and draw a picture of what it looks like viewed through the concave lens. Draw your observations in the space provided below.

Data & Observations

e *viewed through concave lens*   e *viewed through convex lens*

How Come, Huh?

The shape of the lens bends the light as it passes through the water. When held at the proper distance, the lens makes the object look bigger, or magnified. If you continue to move the lens up or down, you will notice the clarity or focus changes and the image becomes inverted. Our eyes invert images onto the back of the retina.

Science Fair Extensions

54. Research other kinds of lenses and how light moves through them. In particular, compare a Fresnel lens to a traditional concave or convex lens. Also, determine how bifocal lenses are made, what they do, who uses them and why. See if you can construct your own model of all of these types of lenses and then adapt them to a specific use.

55. Find instruments that use lenses. Identify what the purpose of the instrument is and how the lens is used to assist the researcher. Examples that may get you started: lighthouse lights, telescopes, cameras, glasses, microscopes, endoscopes, and fiber-optic cables that are inserted into arteries to examine heart patients.

56. Experiment with combinations of concave and convex lenses. Build an apparatus that will allow you to demonstrate how the light moves through these combinations of lenses. Try to determine if there is any possible use for the combinations you have created.

CONVEX LENS

A convex lens bends the light image outward, expanding the appearance of the image you see.

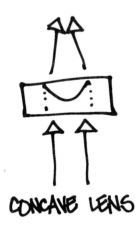

CONCAVE LENS

A concave lens bends the light image inward, reducing the appearance of the image you see.

Inverse Square Law

The Experiment

The farther away we get from a source of light the dimmer it appears. That makes perfect sense. Think about two lampposts, one nearby and the other a couple of blocks away. The lamppost directly overhead is going to seem much brighter than the lamppost down the street, even though they are exactly the same brightness. The inverse square law gives us a mathematical formula for calculating the intensity of the light that strikes a surface.

Materials

1   Ruler
1   Index Card
1   Pair of Scissors or Knife
1   Flashlight (Mini-Maglite® works best)
1   Sheet of Graph Paper, half-inch squares
1   Pencil

Procedure

1. Measure and cut a one-half inch by one-half inch square hole in the center of the index card.

2. Unscrew the reflector on the Mini-Maglite®. When the reflector is removed, the light will come on and stay on.

3. Darken the room and, using the illustration as a guide, place the light 1 inch from the hole and shine the light from the flashlight through that hole onto the graph paper.

4. Without moving the light or the index card, experiment with moving the graph paper away from the index card to fill and illuminate different numbers of squares listed. As you experiment, fill in the data table below. Be sure to measure in inches.

Observations

Number of Squares Illumin.	1	4	9	16
Distance from Index Card (in.)				

How Come, Huh?

As the graph paper was moved to a distance of 1 inch from the card, a single square should have been illuminated. When the graph paper was moved to 2 inches, 4 squares were illuminated, and at 3 inches 9 squares appeared lit. A pretty clear pattern has been established. The area that is illuminated (the number of squares that are lit) is the square of the distance. Or, if A = the area illuminated and d = the distance from the index card to the graph paper, then. . .

$$A = d^2$$

As the total area that is illuminated with light increases, the intensity of that light, the amount of power per area, decreases by the inverse of this formula. The same amount of light is shared over a larger area. Mathematically it looks like this: $P = 1/d^2$.

Science Fair Extensions

57. Repeat the experiment with perfboard and counting holes.
58. Change the size of the hole to 1 inch and test the results.

Kaleidoscope Eyes

The Experiment

There are toys that have rather fancy lenses in them to create optical illusions that are entertaining. You are going to attempt to use one of these as a "transplanted" eye and perform some simple tasks.

Materials

1   Kaleidoscope
1   Toy Ball
1   Pencil and Piece of Paper
1   Assistant

Procedure

1. Hold the kaleidoscope up to your eye, close the other eye, and look around the room. You should see multiple images of everything you look at.

2. Now try doing a couple of simple things while holding the kaleidescope to one eye: walk across a room; write your name in the box below; have your assistant toss you a toy ball so you can catch it.

How Come, Huh?

There are multiple lenses all packed onto one surface. As the image of the toy enters the front of the lens it is split into 12, 16, 24, and sometimes over 100 different lens faces, producing that many images. This, in fact, is how the compound eye found in most insects behaves. Now you know why it is so hard to whap a fly. It sees all 184 of you coming at once.

Science Fair Extensions

59. Do some research and make a kaleidoscope of your own.

Big Idea 10

Light can be bent as it passes through certain materials. The amount it is bent is called the index of refraction and varies from material to material.

Lincoln's Mystery

The Experiment

Light, like sound and heat, travels through different materials at different speeds. In fact, when light travels from one material into another material, it usually either slows down or speeds up. This change in speed is caused by the direction that the light travels in the new material.

This experiment takes advantage of that change in direction, also called the index of refraction, to create an interesting optical illusion.

Materials

2   Opaque Drinking Glasses
1   Penny
   Water
2   Eyes

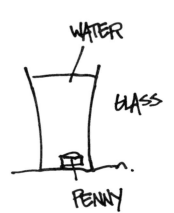

Procedure

1. Fill one glass with water.

2. Plunk the penny in the bottom of the empty glass. Start out by looking into the cup with the penny clearly in your view. Slowly back away from the cup, watching the penny at all times, until the penny disappears from your field of view.

3. Without moving your head, pick up the second glass that is full of water and slowly add it to the glass with the penny. You will notice that as the water level increases, the virtual image of the penny comes back into full view.

How Come, Huh?

In the first case the cup is empty, and the light image of the penny is reflected straight up into the air. There is nothing to get in its way and bend it around. As a consequence, if you do not have a direct line of sight you will not see the penny.

In the second instance, the light from the penny is traveling more slowly through the water. When it leaves the water and enters the air, it not only picks up speed but also gets bent, or refracted, in the process. The bending of the light allows you to see the virtual image of the penny, even though your line of sight is off the mark a bit.

Science Fair Extensions

60. Determine a way to measure the angle that the virtual image of the penny occurs and experiment with different liquids. Measure the angle of refraction and compare that to the index of refraction for that liquid as well as to the molecular shape and density.

61. Measure the depth of the liquid and compare it to the percentage of the virtual image that is seen. Determine a mathematical model that describes how the two are related.

Broken Pencils

The Experiment

A perfectly healthy pencil will be placed in a clear drinking glass. Normal everyday tap water will be added to the same glass. All of sudden you notice that the pencil is broken. Split in two. Defective, if you will. Manufacturing problem or optical illusion? You decide.

Materials

2   Clear Drinking Glasses
1   Pencil
    Water
2   Eyes

Procedure

1. Fill one of the clear drinking glasses with water.

2. Place the pencil in the other, empty drinking glass and take a peek at it from the side. Draw a picture of what you see in the space on the next page.

3. Slowly add water to the glass that contains the pencil. As the water level increases observe what happens to the image of the pencil. Draw a picture of the image you see when the cup is half full and again when it is completely full.

4. When you are done with your observations, empty the cup and examine the pencil.

Data & Observations

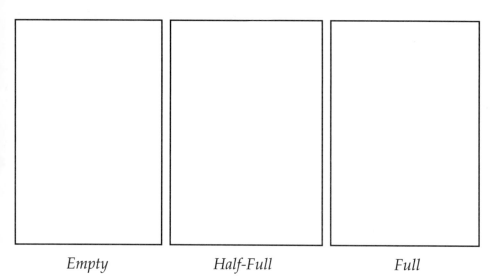

Empty Half-Full Full

How Come, Huh?

When light travels through the water and hits the air, it bends. The amount it bends is measured and called the index of refraction. It is determined by the optical density of the material. The denser the material, the slower the light moves, and the greater the angle that the light wave is bent.

Science Fair Extensions

62. Observe and measure the index of refraction for several different materials. Place the liquids in order of density and see if that matches the index of refraction you created.

63. Experiment with different materials and see if the index of refraction is in any way connected to the items being used.

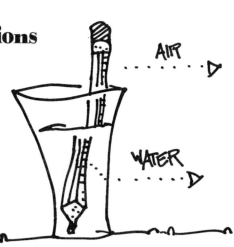

Spearing Washers

The Experiment

When light passes through a material, it usually gets bent. If the material is water, the light gets bent quite a bit and produces some interesting optical illusions. You are going to construct the apparatus pictured below and play a game called Spear the Washer. This game takes advantage of the refractive index of water to create some problems for your coodination.

Materials

1 12 to 16 oz. Glass
1 12" Length of String
1 Medium-Size Washer
1 Plastic Straw
1 Bamboo Skewer
   Water

Procedure

1. Fill a large glass with water.

2. Tie a medium-size washer to one end of the string. Tie the other end of the string to the plastic straw, without the wrapper of course, and lower the washer into the glass of water. Roll the straw, raising the washer until it is suspended about an inch above the bottom of the glass.

3. Push the straw to the edge of the glass so that the washer is close to one side of the container.

4. Now close one eye. Watch the skewer through the top surface of the water and do your very best to slide the bamboo skewer through the center of the washer. No looking through the side, top of the water only.

5. Having a coordination problem? Blame it on refraction!

How Come, Huh?

Light travels differently through different materials. The refraction (bending) of light occurs as it goes from the air to the water in the container. When you think you have the skewer lined up exactly. . . you really do, but you have it lined up looking through the air. You are being tricked because you see the image as it passes through water.

Science Fair Extensions

64. Place a pencil or straw in a glass of water and look at it from different angles. The item will appear bent or broken where it enters the water. Draw pictures or take photographs of the same item being placed in several different liquids. Compare the angle of refraction for each one.

65. Build "The Big Bender." Find a tall 10-gallon aquarium or old water bottle that you can chop the top off of and set up a large-scale replica of the same experiment. Challenge your friends or siblings to come up and spear the washer.

66. Recreate the experiment but use different liquids. Try oil, vinegar, ammonia, distilled water, mineral oil. Create an experiment where you can actually measure the refractive index of each liquid and rank them from the most to the least refraction.

Ghost Crystals

The Experiment

Ghost crystals get their name because when they become wet they are virtually invisible. This does not have anything to do with any mystical properties, witchcraft, voodoo, or other assorted pastimes. It is just straight science that demonstrates the difference between transparent and opaque materials and takes advantage of the index of refraction.

Materials

1 Bottle of Ghost Crystals (Sodium Polyacrylamide)
1 Sheet of Paper
1 Pencil
1 Petri Dish Half
1 Glass of Water
1 Assistant

Procedure

1. Place the petri dish half on the sheet of paper and draw a circle around the outside of the dish.

2. Remove the dish and write a message on the paper inside of the outline of the dish like, "I love polymers," "Hey, I'm not dressed yet!" or "What are you lookin' at?" Have fun and think of something that will make someone smile with surprise.

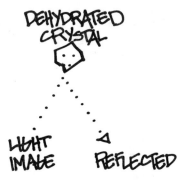

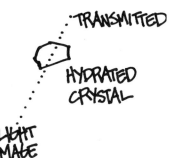

3. Place the petri dish back on the message. Sprinkle sodium polyacrylamide (ghost) crystals on the dish so that they completely cover the message.

4. Ask your assistant to come over to the dish and look down and try to read the message. When he gives up, have him pour the water gently into the dish. The message will be revealed as the crystals absorb the water and become transparent.

How Come, Huh?

When the crystals absorb the water, they swell and become transparent, allowing the light to pass through. The image was obscured by the opaque, dehydrated crystals that reflected the light image. It can now be seen without any problem at all.

Science Fair Extensions

67. Tie a thread around a large crystal. Lower the crystal into a glass of water, and it appears to disappear. Pull it out, and it reappears. Come up with a good story and have fun with your friends.

Glass Rod Repair Shop

The Experiment

This lab is a fun zinger and a great way to introduce refraction and reflection. As it turns out, glass and some commercial types of corn oil have the same index of refraction. In other words, light bends at the same angle when it passes through either one. The interesting side bar is that it makes the glass objects inside the corn oil nearly invisible to the naked eye.

Materials

1   Pint of Wesson™ Corn Oil
1   Roll of Masking Tape
1   Black Pen
1   Drinking Glass or 500 mL Beaker
2   Glass Rods
1   Hammer
1   Dishcloth
1   Glass Eyedropper
1   Magnifying Glass

Procedure

1. Before your audience shows up, fill a drinking glass or beaker with Wesson™ corn oil. Using a piece of masking tape, make a label that says, "Glass Rod Restorer." Place the label across the middle of the drinking glass. Place one of the two glass rods inside the glass with the corn oil. Make sure that it is completely submerged under the corn oil.

2. When your audience arrives, ask one member to peer into the glass and look to see if there is anything there. You don't want to hand them the glass because they may catch a faint glimpse of the rod at the bottom, so simply hold the container at eye level and move through the observation quickly.

3. After the appropriate inspection period, hold a glass rod up and ask one of your friends to examine it. Upon confirmation of its entirety, wrap the rod in the dish cloth and smash it with the hammer. The smaller the pieces the better. Be sure you wrap the glass rod thoroughly so none of the broken pieces fly out and hit anyone.

4. Empty the pieces into the drinking glass with the corn oil labeled "Glass Rod Restorer." Place the dishcloth over the beaker and inform your friends that you have procured a special solution that miraculously repairs broken glass. Really.

5. After sufficient propaganda on your part, remove the cloth and reach into the jar to retrieve a whole glass rod to the astonished looks of your comrades and audience. Wipe the rod off and pass it around. If they ask you to repeat your performance, politely decline.

Glass Rod Repair Shop

6. After the applause has died down, take a glass eyedropper and insert it halfway into the oil. It will appear to have a ghostly image, but will not be invisible until you squeeze the bulb and draw the oil up into the tube. When this happens, it appears as though the eyedropper has disappeared.

7. And for your final experiment, gently dip a magnifying glass into the oil. You will notice that, unlike air or water, the light is not refracted and magnified.

How Come, Huh?

There are several parts to this explanation.

1. When light travels through the air and strikes the glass surface at an angle, a portion of the light is reflected. This is why we see the outline of the rod if it is placed in water or even waved around in the air.

2. The rest of the light enters the glass rod, but as it does so, it is bent, or refracted, at an angle. The reason it does this is the light slows down when it goes from the air into the glass. In fact, all materials slow down light particles. This slowing is described as the index of refraction. The slower the light travels, the higher the index of refraction. Check out the first illustration on the next page.

3. In the case of the stirring rod and the Wesson™ oil, their indices of refraction are almost identical, which means that as the light passes through the oil and into the glass, it does not bend or refract enough to be detected by the human eye. See the second illustration on the next page.

4. When you placed the glass eyedropper into the oil, it was full of air. The light entered the oil, zipped through the glass and then hit the air. The index of refraction for the oil and the glass were the same, but the index of refraction for the air was different. So the light sped up and was bent, and as a consequence we could see the inside of the eyedropper. As soon as the oil entered the eyedropper, the index of refraction became uniform and the eyedropper was very hard to see.

Most materials bend light rays as they pass through them. The amount they bend the light is called the index of refraction and is measured as an angle.

Science Fair Ideas

68. Try other glass items. Solid objects seem to work better than hollow items like test tubes or small beakers.

69. Rumor has it that heavy mineral oil also works well with glass. This can be acquired from your local pharmacy; it is sold as a laxative. If that does not work, try mixing heavy and light mineral oil.

If the index of refraction is equal for both objects, the light appears to pass straight through.

70. Experiment with plastic and other liquids. See if you can find a liquid that refracts at the same angle.

71. Rumor has it that temperature also affects this experiment. Heat and cool the oil to different temperatures and observe the results. Create a model to explain why the temperature (density) of the oil would have an effect and use your studies to make predictions about other liquids.

Shoebox Refraction

The Experiment

Some magicians can seemingly bend a spoon with only their mind. Many people can bend the truth without thinking about it. In this activity you will bend something you cannot touch. . . light. By using a glass jar to work as a convex lens, you will see and manipulate the light to learn about its bendable quality, called the index of refraction.

Materials

1   Piece of White Paper
1   Shoebox (lid not necessary)
1   Pair of Scissors
1   Metric Ruler
1   Baby Food Jar
1   Pencil
1   Flashlight
     Water, 3 oz.
     Air, 3 oz.
     Oil, 3 oz.

Procedure

1. Place a piece of white paper in the bottom of the shoebox. This will allow you to trace the beams of light as they travel to, pass through, and leave the baby food jar.

2. With your shoebox open side up, cut two vertical slits about 2 centimeters apart in the middle of one end. Each of the slits should be about as thick as a nickel.

3. Place the jar in the middle of the shoebox and trace a circle around the base of the jar so that you can replace it in the exact same spot each time. Turn the flashlight on and place it about 10 centimeters from the two slits that you cut. You should see two distinct beams of light entering the shoebox.

4. Trace the beams of light on the paper as they travel through the baby food jar full of air.

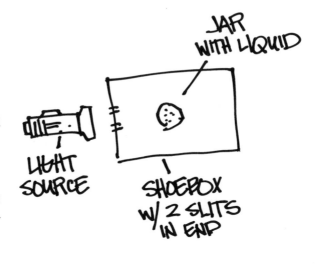

5. Fill the jar with water and repeat the experiment, marking the pathways of the beams of light on the paper.

6. Finally, fill the baby food jar with oil and repeat the experiment a third time. Compare the index of refraction for each medium and determine which one bends light the most.

Data & Observations

Copy the paper that was on the inside of the shoebox, showing where the baby food jar was located and how the three sets of beams of light traveled.

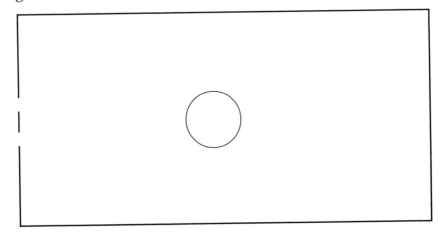

Shoebox Refraction

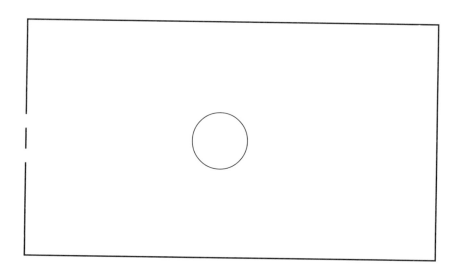

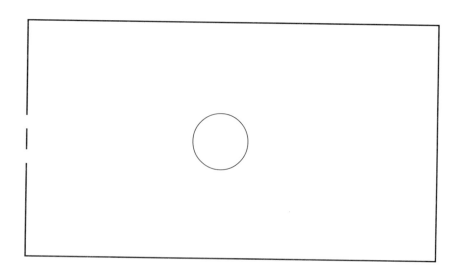

How Come, Huh?

Why does light bend? As light hits a transparent surface and goes through it, like the glass jar filled with water, the light bends and changes its direction (see illustration below). This light bending is called refraction. This refracting of light varies upon the angle at which the light hits the object.

Science Fair Extensions

72. Repeat the experiment using a single slot and see if your measurements are the same. Try three slots with the new slot pointing directly into the middle of the baby food jar.

73. Continue to vary the liquids in the baby food jar. Rank the liquids by density, molecular weight, and index of refraction. Is there a correlation between any of these three?

74. Temperature affects the density of a liquid. If it is cold, it becomes more dense. The atoms in the liquid slow down and are packed more closely together. By contrast, the warmer the liquid, the less dense. What effect, if any, does this have on the ability of the liquid to refract light? Be sure to set up controls and very carefully measure the angle of refraction that is produced.

75. Instead of using liquids, try transparent solids like glass, plastic, and acrylic. Measure single and double sections.

Most materials bend light rays as they pass through them. The amount they bend the light is called the index of refraction and is measured as an angle.

Big Idea 11

Light can be reflected off the surface of a material. The incident angle of light always equals the reflected angle of light.

Bouncing Light

The Experiment

A plane mirror is used to confirm that photons of light travel in a straight line. Mathematical measurements of the angle of incidence (flashlight to mirror) and the angle of reflection (mirror to wherever the light reflects to) are observed and recorded. This lab demands precise technique and focus, always qualities to strive for.

CARD W/HOLE

TAPE

Materials

1   Protractor
1   Pair of Scissors or Knife
1   Metric Ruler
1   Index Card
1   Flashlight
1   Roll of Tape
1   Plane (Flat) Mirror
1   Sheet of white paper

FLASHLIGHT

Procedure

1. In the very back of this book there is a protractor that you can photocopy, cut out, and

Bouncing Light

use to measure the angles of the bouncing light. You can also use a commercial protractor available where school supplies are sold.

2. Cut a narrow slit in the index card, approximately 1 mm, and tape it to the front of the flashlight. Use the illustration on the previous page as a guide.

3. Arrange the mirror, sheet of paper, and the flashlight with the card so that it resembles the configuration pictured below. Once the room is darkened, you should be able to see a thin beam of light emerging from the slot in the card, traveling across the sheet of paper, and bouncing off the mirror. Work with the setup until you get this effect.

4. Once you get the thin beam of light without too much difficulty, practice sending a beam of light across the sheet of paper from various angles, hitting the mirror right at dead center, and finding that exact same light beam reflecting out across the other side of the paper protractor. This requires a talented marksman, so take your time and practice. Resist all temptations to shoot light rays around the room.

5. Once you get the hang of shooting a beam of light at the mirror and getting it to reflect, fill in the data table on the next page.

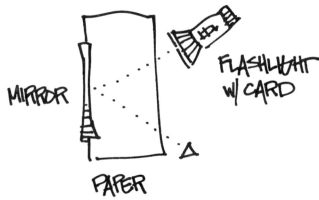

MIRROR

FLASHLIGHT w/ CARD

PAPER

Data Table

Fill in the data table below:

Trial #	Angle In	Angle Out
1	45°	
2	15°	
3	35°	
4		20°
5		75°

How Come, Huh?

This one is short and sweet. The angle of the incident (incoming) beam of light always equals the angle of the reflected (outgoing) beam of light.

Science Fair Extensions

76. The angle in is actually called the angle of incidence or i^r and the angle out is usually referred to as the angle of reflection or i^o. Design a gizmo that allows you to rotate the beam of light easily and also allows you to measure the angle of incidence and the angle of reflection easily and quickly.

77. Substitute other reflective surfaces for the mirror.

Up Periscope!

The Experiment

We are going to take advantage of the fact that light bounces and can be reflected to make a toy that will allow you to see around corners, over fences, and into rooms without anyone seeing you. Who says science doesn't have any fun applications?

Materials

1   Milk Carton, Cardboard, Pint
    Water
1   Paper Towel
1   Pair of Scissors or Sharp Knife
2   Plane Mirrors
1   Roll of Masking Tape

Procedure

1. Rinse the milk carton out to remove any excess milk and dry the inside with a paper towel.

2. Using the pattern, on the opposite page, cut horizontal rectangles, 2" tall and 3" wide, on opposite sides of the milk carton. Cut one rectangle near the top and the other near the bottom.

3. Again using the pattern, make diagonal cuts large enough to hold the mirrors near the top and bottom of the milk carton.

4. Slide the top mirror into the top set of diagonal cuts with the mirrored side facing down. Slide the bottom mirror into the slots with the mirrored side facing up.

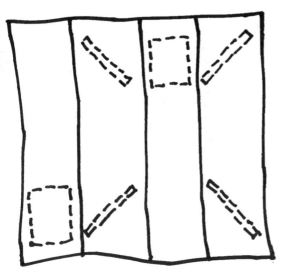

5. Find a corner to peek around, a fence to peep over, or a window to gaze into and experiment using your periscope. You may have to adjust the mirrors a little, but if you cut the diagonals at exactly 45° angles you will see the image that is reflected around the corner.

How Come, Huh?

We are taking advantage of the fact that light bounces and reflects off shiny surfaces. The light image enters the box at the top of your periscope. It strikes the mirror, reflects down to the other mirror, and bounces over to your eye. The illustration at the bottom of the page should be of considerable help.

Science Fair Ideas

78. Experiment with the length of the periscope. Try making one using a very long mailing tube and see if you can use it to see over very tall fences.

79. Design a periscope that incorporates three mirrors to see around corners. Draw your design first and then build it. Be sure to measure the angle of incidence and the angle of reflection for each time the light would bounce inside the instrument.

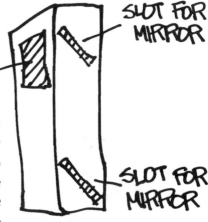

TOP VIEWING HOLE

SLOT FOR MIRROR

SLOT FOR MIRROR

To Infinity & Beyond

The Experiment

We know that light can be reflected off a smooth surface like polished metal or a glass mirror. This lab will create the illusion of multiple images that appear to go on for an infinite number of repetitions.

Materials

2   Plane Mirrors
1   Lump of Clay
1   Small Object, Bow, Key, or Action Figure

Procedure

1. Take the clay and make four small balls. Place two balls on the side of each mirror and squish them so that they support the mirrors.

2. Place the two mirrors about six inches apart. They should be almost directly facing one another. Place the small object of choice between the two mirrors and look at the image that is created as the light bounces between them.

How Come, Huh?

The image of the small object is reflected off one mirror at a very small angle to the other mirror. Since the angle of incidence equals the angle of reflection, the second mirror bounces the image back to the first mirror at the same, small angle. This back-and-forth bouncing creates the illusion that you see in this experiment.

The illustration to the right helps you understand what you see. The solid lines are the actual light waves that are bouncing back and forth between the mirrors, and the dotted lines represent the virtual waves that are perceived by your brain. It is these virtual images that create the illusion of the object between the mirrors repeating on into infinity.

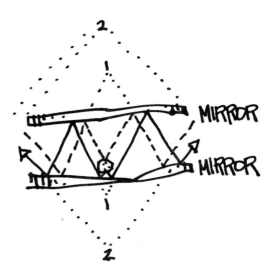

Science Fair Extensions

80. There are several other ways to recreate this experiment. One is to rub the silver off the back of a mirror creating a hole you can look through. Another way to see between the mirrors is to take one of the mirrors to a plastics store and have them cut a hole in the center. That way you can look directly through the mirror into the illusion.

81. Another option is to cut and place sponges between the two mirrors and hold everything together using rubber bands. Then, when you look in the mirrors you can adjust the position of the object and the perspective you see by gently squeezing the sponges. The angle between the mirrors will change as the sponges are compressed.

Big Idea 12

Light can enter and be completely reflected inside some objects. When this phenomenon happens, it is called total internal reflection.

The Critical Angle

The Experiment

All right, we know that light will bounce and reflect off a smooth, hard surface. It will even bounce off an irregular surface like aluminum foil that has been crumpled up. But what about transparent materials, like water? If the light strikes the margin of a liquid or film at a high enough angle (called the critical angle), a portion of the light will be refracted into the new medium. If the angle is not high enough, the light will be completely reflected back into the liquid. This phenomenon is called total internal reflection. Transcendental meditation optional.

Materials

1   10 Gallon Aquarium
10 Gallons of Water
1   Powdered Milk, 1 Tsp.
1   Flashlight, Maglite™ Works Well
1   Protractor (optional)
1   Table

Procedure

1. Place the aquarium on a table so it is easy to look up at the surface of the water from the underside.

2. Add the 10 gallons of water to the aquarium. Then, add a pinch or two of powdered milk—just enough so that you can see the beam of light when you shine it into the tank.

The Critical Angle

Procedure

3. Darken the room and shine the beam of light through the end of the tank, up onto the bottom surface of the water at an angle of 45 degrees or more. The illustration on the previous page will give you a good idea of what you are trying to accomplish.

ANGLE LESS THAN 49°

ANGLE GREATER THAN 49°

4. Experiment with the angles so that the light strikes the bottom of the surface of the water. You should notice that if the beam strikes the surface between the air and the water at an angle of 49 degrees or less, the light is completely reflected back into the water. If the angle is greater than that, the beam will be split and a portion will refract out into the air and the remainder will be reflected back into the tank.

How Come, Huh?

When the light traveling through the water hits the interface between the air and the water at a high enough angle, it is refracted, or bent, out of the water and into the air. If the angle is shallow enough, the incident beam will bounce off the surface and be nearly 100 percent reflected back into the water. This is called total internal reflection.

Science Fair Extensions

82. Find and compare the critical angle for a number of different liquids and see if they are the same or different.

83. Experiment with the kind of beam and see if that has any effect. Try different colors, shapes, thicknesses, and intensities.

Pouring Light

The Experiment

You are going to pour some light in this experiment. That's right... POUR. As this demonstration begins, your job is to form your own hypothesis as to how in the heck it is being done. Magic is not a good answer, however; if you are doing these labs in order, an idea like total internal reflection may come in handy.

Materials

1 Soup Can with One End Open
1 Hammer
1 Large Nail
1 Flashlight
1 Assistant
   Water
1 Tub or Sink

FLASHLIGHT

#303 SOUP CAN W/WATER

HOLE

WATER STREAM

Procedure

1. Punch a hole on the side of the can, close to the bottom, with the hammer and nail. Test it by putting water in and letting it drain out of the hole. You need a good stream to achieve the best effect.

2. Place your finger over the hole and fill up the soup can with water. Turn your flashlight on and place it over the can so it is shining directly down into the water. Turn off the lights, and move your finger to release the stream of water.

3. As the water flows from the can have your assistant place her index finger into the stream of water. You will see the beam of light illuminated on her fingertip.

How Come, Huh?

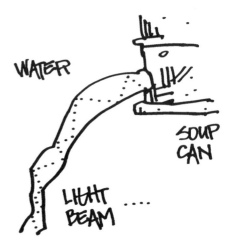

Well ... you have a medium with a high refractive index (the water). It is surrounded by another medium with a lower refractive index (the air). The light is contained within the stream of water coming out of the hole. In order for the light to escape the water, it needs to hit the surface of the stream at an angle of 49 degrees or greater. Since it is hitting it at less than that, it is reflected back into the water stream. This bouncing back and forth inside the stream of water is called total internal reflection and is a product of the light hitting the interface between the air and water at a shallow enough angle that it can't escape.

Science Fair Extensions

84. Repeat the experiment with different liquids. Try cooking oil, rubbing alcohol, soda pop; let your imagination run wild. See which liquids have total internal reflection and which ones don't.

85. You know that water demonstrates total internal reflection, and we tell you that a fiber-optics cable does as well. What about similar characteristics in plant fibers, animal adaptations, or minerals? Do your research.

Big Idea 13

Waves can bounce off surfaces and interfere with other light waves. This is called wave interference, which can be either constructive or destructive.

© 2000 • B. K. Hixson

Bubble Wave Wars

The Experiment

A soap film appears to be one thin surface to the naked eye. When light strikes it at an angle, it creates some very interesting patterns and colors because it is really two surfaces, a front and a back. When light is reflected off both surfaces, they tend to either compliment or cancel each other. This is called constructive and destructive interference.

Materials

2 Straws
1 30" Length of Cotton String
1 Small Tub
$\frac{2}{3}$ Cup of Dawn™ Liquid Soap
1 Gallon of Water
1 Tablespoon of Glycerine

Procedure

1. Thread the two straws on to the length of cotton string. Tie the string ends together and rotate the knot so that it is inside one of the straws.

2. Next, you will need to mix up a batch of soap solution. All bubble experts recommend using Dawn™ liquid soap as the base. No one knows the secret ingredient that Proctor & Gamble puts in there, but it makes incredible bubbles. Mix the following ingredients in the tub and let it sit overnight for best results:

1   Gallon of Water
1   Tablespoon of Glycerine
⅔   Cup of Dawn™, Liquid Soap

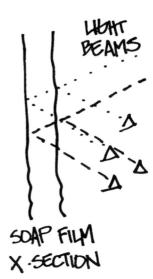

LIGHT BEAMS

3. Hold the two straws together and dip them into the soap solution. Lift them out together and slowly separate them to create a large soap sheet or film. Observe the colors, wiggle the straws back and forth, and blow on the sheet to make bulges.

SOAP FILM
X-SECTION

How Come, Huh?

The soap film is actually three layers, two layers of soap molecules trapping a layer of water in between. Some of the light is reflected off the front surface and more of the light is reflected off the back surface. When these two reflections pig pile on one another, sometimes the waves amplify and get larger and sometimes they cancel each other out. This is called wave interference.

As the water drains between the two layers of soap, it changes the thickness of the film and the way the light is reflected. If the waves are destructive, different colors are produced. Start with the three basic colors make up white light: red, blue, and green. If there is destructive, interference that removes blue, then: white light - blue light = red + green = yellow. So when you see yellows on the film you are looking at a destructive interference that was created by wiping out the blue waves.

Science Fair Extensions

86. Experiment with different colored backgrounds and see if it affects the color patterns you see.

87. Try three-dimensional soap patterns and see if multiple layers of bubble film produce the same effect that a single layer does.

Rainbow Sandwich

The Experiment

If we just pulled you away from making and playing with bubbles, this lab will make a whole lot more sense. In the previous lab we told you that there were actually three layers that produced the interference patterns and all of the beautiful colors. In this lab you will be able to actually see the layers as you assemble them.

Materials

2   Sheets of Plexiglas™, .64 mm or .33 cm thick, 1 foot sq.
1   Bottle of Rubbing Alcohol
1   Soft Cloth
1   Sheet of Black Paper
1   Roll of Black Tape
1   Strong Source of White Light

Procedure

1. Remove the protective paper on the back of the Plexiglas™ squares and wipe them down with the soft cloth soaked in alcohol.

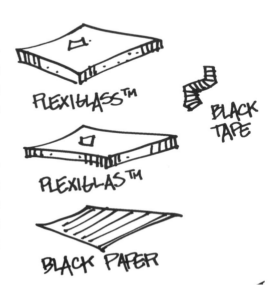

FLEXIGLASS™

BLACK TAPE

PLEXIGLAS™

BLACK PAPER

2. Place the black paper on the table and then place the two Plexiglas™ squares on top of the paper. Tape all three pieces together using the black tape.

3. You now have three layers: Plexiglas™, air, and Plexiglas™. Hold the color sandwich in your hands and gently bend the sheets back and forth. You will see colors appear and disappear as constructive and destructive wave patterns are created by changing the thickness of the layers.

How Come, Huh?

When you hold the sandwich in white light, the beams strike the top of the first plate and a little light is reflected, just like the bubble film. Most of the light travels through the Plexiglas™ but some of it gets reflected when it hits the thin layer of air inside the two plates. Finally, more beams of light bounce off the back of the second layer of Plexiglas™. All of these waves bouncing around have a tendency to run into one another. When this happens, it can either have an additive effect (constructive interference) or a cancelling effect (destructive interference).

As with the soap film, when one of the three primary colors that make up white light is cancelled it produces other colors. The interference patterns that you see depend on the thickness between the two plates, and the pattern is actually a very, very thin 3D topographic map.

Science Fair Ideas

88. Compare the patterns that you see when you use different thicknesses of Plexiglas™.

89. What happens when you add water between the pieces of Plexiglas™? How about oil? Does this lab work if you use regular old glass?

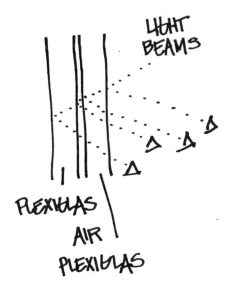

Big Idea 14

Optical illusions are light images that are reflected to the eye and trick the brain into thinking it is seeing something it is not.

Color-Mixing Tops

The Experiment

If you spin a black-and-white Holstein (cow) around and around in a farmer's field, will you begin to see a cow of many colors? No, but you might see stars if the cow regains balance and takes after you. Besides, cows are too big to spin. Let's use black-and-white patterns on a disk instead. In addition to spinning different patterns of black and white, you can also experiment with combinations of colors to get them to mix and produce secondary and tertiary colors as well. Crayons up!

Materials

3   Index Cards, No Lines
1   Empty #303 Soup Can or Other Round Object
1   Set of Black-and-White Patterns
1   Pair of Scissors
1   Hole Punch
1   Set of Crayons or Colored Pencils
1   Spinner Top

Procedure

CRAYON

1. Place the soup can on the index card and draw as many circles as you possibly can on each card; then cut them out. Make a hole in the very center of each disk using the hole punch.

PAPER DISK

TOP

2. Create the first four color combinations of disks listed on the data table on the next page. Color half the disk one color and the other half the other color. Place the disk on the spinner top and give it a spin. Record the resulting color. If there are more than two starting colors, divide the disk equally.

Color-Mixing Tops

Data & Observations

Disk	Colors	Resultant Color(s)
1	Blue/Red	
2	Blue/Yellow	
3	Red/Yellow	
4	Green/Yellow/Orange	
5		
6		
7		
8		

3. Once you have tried the first four combinations, then experiment with other color combinations of your own design. Be sure to fill in the data table above with your experiments and observations.

4. Using the pattern disks pictured to the right, either copy or photocopy the patterns and put them on your spinner top (after you have removed the colored disks, of course). As you spin the disks, you will find that certain bands of color will appear at different locations on the disk or different illusions are created.

5. Spin each disk and record your observations in the data table below. The blank disks (E and F) are for you to use to create combinations of colors or new patterns that you would like to explore.

Disk	Resultant Color(s) or Illusion
A	
B	
C	
D	

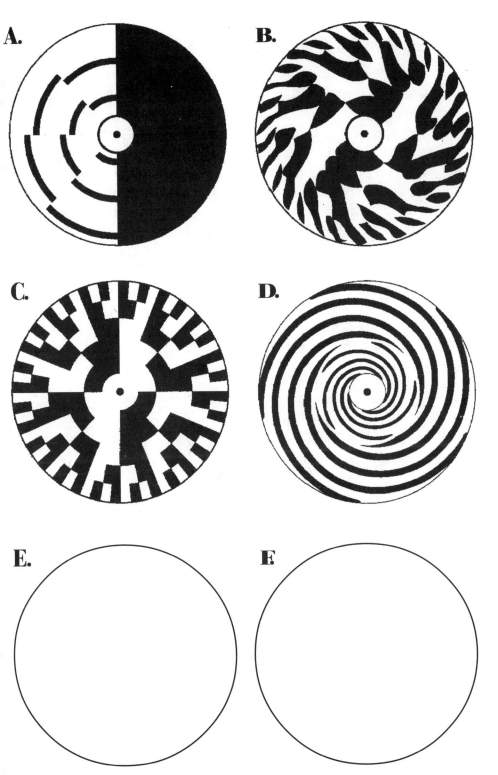

A.

B.

C.

D.

E.

F.

Color-Mixing Tops

How Come, Huh?

Why you see colors on the black-and-white-pattern disks is still somewhat of a mystery, but scientists believe it has to do with the cones that are located in the back of your eyeball.

There are three kinds of cones that collect each of the colors red, green, and blue. They also seem to process the information at different speeds. This is called the *latency time*. For example, red cones are the quickest to collect light information. They also dump the information to the brain the quickest. This is called the *persistence of response* time. Blue cones, on the other hand, are the slowest to collect and the slowest to send the information on. This helps to begin to explain why our brains think they see colors.

As the disk spins, your eye sees alternating flashes of black and white. As the flashes of white light (made up of all the colors of the rainbow) hit your cones, the cones do not collect the colors at the same rate. Nor do they send that color information on to the brain at the same rate. It is kind of like the difference between eating buttered, salted popcorn by the handful versus eating a piece of popcorn, then salting your tongue, and then smearing a patty of butter across your tongue. You have the same basic components but much different perception by your brain.

Science Fair Extensions

90. You can repeat the experiment and get a little more sophisticated by enlarging these disks on a copy machine and then attaching them to a variable speed drill. When you squeeze the trigger of the drill, the disks start to spin, and you will see all kinds of colors.

91. The results you see are also affected by the direction in which the pattern is spinning. If you have a variable-speed drill, it probably also has a reverse. Try the pattern in the opposite direction.

92. The thickness of the lines also makes a big difference in the colors that you do or do not see. Experiment with the line thickness and the ability to see colors using the basic disk pattern A.

Mouse in the House

The Experiment

This is picture blending at its best! When you sit in front of the tube and watch cartoons on Saturday morning, you are experiencing something called persistence of vision. Don't worry! It's nothing to call the doctor about, it just means that a cartoon image that you see will remain in your vision for one tenth of a second after it is gone. Cartoons are made by putting lots and lots of frames of pictures together. Therefore, when the frames are flashed before you, they blend with the previous one to give you the illusion of movement. Try this easy Mouse in the House and then try creating your own.

Materials

1 4" by 6" Index Card
1 Straw
1 Stapler
1 Roll of Scotch Tape

Procedure

1. Divide the 4" by 6" card in half visually and draw the pictures of the mouse on one half and the house on the other.

2. Fold the card in half, picture side out, and staple it shut. Slide the straw up the middle of the card and tape it in place on both the top and the bottom of the card.

3. Hold the straw between your palms and roll it quickly back and forth. Look at the picture that is created.

Mouse in the House

How Come, Huh?

So how does all this fancy imagery work, you ask? An image remains in your sight for one-tenth of a second after it disappears. This is called *persistence of vision*. When you are rolling the straw between your hands, you see one picture. Then in the next tenth of a second, you see a different picture. The two pictures are blended together.

Cartoons are made by drawing or creating one frame at a time. Each frame is slightly different from the previous one. When the frames are flashed before our eyes, the previous image persists, or sticks around, for one-tenth of a second while the next one is presented to us. This creates the illusion of frames blending together and the image appears to be in motion.

Science Fair Extensions

93. Another way to create this illusion is to cut circular disks. Punch two small holes on either side and thread a piece of string through each hole. The disk has a mouse on one side and a house on the other. Wind the strings tightly. When you pull the strings, the disk spins, creating the same illusion.

94. Create a cartoon flip book. These use the same principle of persistence of vision that the mouse in the house does. Decide what sequence of events you want to depict, a girl running, a man catching a ball, a dog chasing a mailman, something entertaining.

Start at the back of a small pad of paper and draw the first picture in the sequence. Next page, next illustration, and so on. When you are done, grab all of the pages and start flipping them as evenly as you can. If everything went well, you'll see a cartoon in motion.

Optical Illusion Gallery

The Experiment

This is a collection of optical illusions. As a general rule, these illusions work because we develop ideas or notions of how our world should appear through experience. When we see something new, we base our evaluation on what we already know.

Several of these illusions are based on classical line drawings that have been around for a long time and use the relationship of lines and space to create the illusion. Illusion 1 is the perfect example. You are asked to determine which line is the longest and which is the shortest. If you take a ruler and measure each of the lines you may be surprised at what you find.

Illusions 2, 3, and 4 are also created by adding reference lines or objects that trick the eye into thinking that the distances have changed or are in some way different. Again, a ruler will bring the truth to light.

The 5th illusion is simply a test of how you look at a picture. It was created by the cartoonist W.H. Breenan in 1915, and some psychologists will tell you that it provides insight into how you view the world.

Finally, the last illusion is called a *perceived depth image*. When you finally get it in focus, it looks like a three-dimensional image coming up out of the page toward you. In reality it is an illusion created by interfering messages sent by each eye to the brain at the same time. The way it works is that you train your eyes to focus beyond the image by looking at the two dots. This produces a *virtual focal point* in back of the page. Once the eyes are focused on this virtual focal point, they each send the pattern of black lines and white lines to the brain. The brain's job is to sort the information from each eye and plop it together to make a coherent image out of the data. It just so happens that when you overlap these two patterns a virtual three-dimensional image is created in the brain.

Have fun taking these basic ideas and using them as the starting point for creating your own illusions.

Optical Illusion Gallery

Procedure

Examine each of the optical illusions below and try to determine the correct answer simply by looking at the illusion. After you have selected one, get a ruler and measure to see if you are correct if it is appropriate.

1. Look at the five lines below. List the lines from longest to shortest.

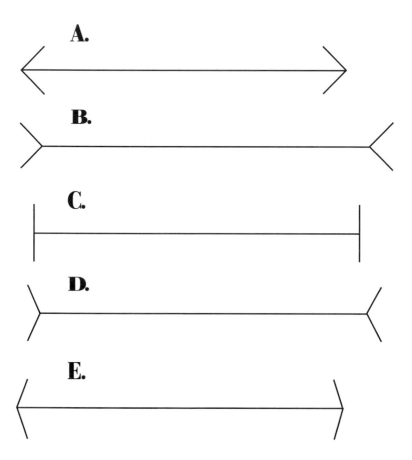

2. Is the letter B below closer to letters A or to C?

3. Which circle is larger in diameter, A or B?

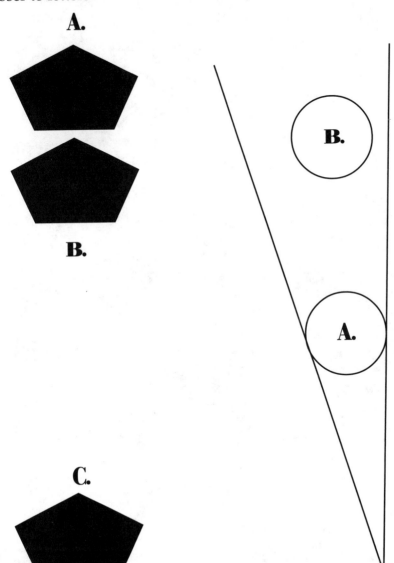

A.

B.

C.

B.

A.

Optical Illusion Gallery

4. Which circle is larger in diameter, A or B?

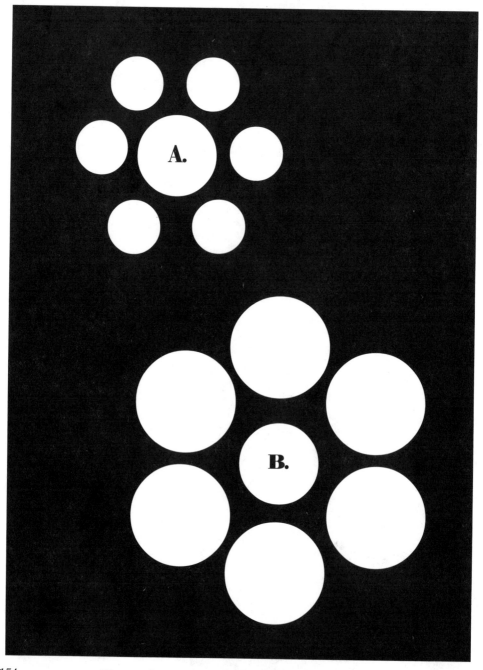

5. This illusion is guided by your initial perception of the image you see. When you look at the picture below you will either see an old lady looking down and toward you or a young lady also looking down but away.

Look at the illustration below and trace the outline of the old lady's nose with red pencil. Outline the nose of the young lady with a green pencil.

Optical Illusion Gallery

6. This pattern is called a PDI, which is short for "Perceived Depth Image." It is created by teaching your eyes to focus behind the illustration, mixing the line patterns sent to your brain where they are interpreted as a 3D image.

To see the perceived depth image, look at the two dots at the bottom of the design. Cross your eyes while looking at them and a third dot will appear. Keep your eyes crossed and focused on the third dot in the center of the other two until they become comfortable in this position. Keeping your eyes crossed, shift your gaze up to the pattern and the images will gradually appear. The pattern is described on page 214.

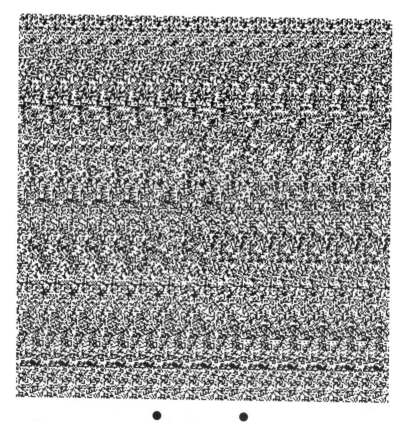

Big Idea 15

Light can be absorbed. When this happens, the object that absorbs the light may experience a temperature increase, color change, or possibly a change of state.

Solar Snapshots

The Experiment

Using light-sensitive paper, you can make snapshot images without a camera. Did you "shutter" with excitement at the thought? Now picture this. . . when the sun-sensitive paper is placed in the sunlight, it will change color. Opaque objects that are placed on the paper will not allow light to pass through and therefore leave the snapshot image. Click!

Materials

1	Sheet of Light-sensitive Paper
3	Small <u>Opaque</u> Objects
1	Sun (free from morning 'til night)
1	Pencil
1	Large Plastic Tub
	Water

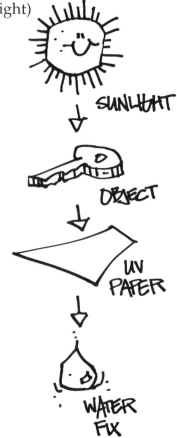

Procedure

1. Collect several opaque objects. These are things that light **cannot** pass through like paper clips, keys, and pencils. Take the black envelope containing the light-sensitive paper and your objects outside into the sunshine.

2. Open the envelope and place the paper, blue side up, in the sunshine. Place opaque objects you've collected on the light-sensitive paper and leave them in the bright sunshine until the paper turns a pale blue. It should take about two minutes, but if you are doing this lab on a cloudy day, it may take a bit longer. DO NOT OVEREXPOSE THE PAPER.

3. Remove the opaque objects. Place the sheet of exposed paper in a tub of water for one minute. When the time is up, take the sheet out of the water and lay it on a flat surface to dry.

How Come, Huh?

The paper you are using is light sensitive. That means if it is exposed to the sun, it will change color. Think back to opaque, translucent, and transparent. If you place an opaque object on the paper, the light will be blocked out so the paper will not change color under that area.

Science Fair Extensions

95. Repeat the experiment but use transparent and translucent objects and see how that affects the images you make. For another alternative, sunblocks are rated for their effectiveness to block ultra-violet rays. Acquire samples of sunblocks with various ratings; 0 (some of the tropical oils have no ability to block UV light), 2, 4, 6, 15, and 45. While you are inside in a dimly lit room, write your name with each of the sunblocks on the light-sensitive paper. Be sure to identify each sample using a pen or pencil. Stick the paper outside and see how they do.

UV Beads

The Experiment

This activity will make you look like the David Copperfield of light and color in the eyes of your friends. You are going to make the invisible visible. Ultraviolet waves are really out there. If you don't believe it, lie outside all day long some hot, sunny July day in your little bikini without sunblock and then immerse yourself in a tub of hot water that same evening. What a wonderful sensation that is! You are feeling the effects of ultraviolet waves on your damaged skin cells. Not to mention the added benefit of looking like a lobster with a little white bathing suit painted on.

The first part of this activity is simply to observe a color change that occurs when the beads absorb ultraviolet light and then radiate visible light. The lab suggests testing the effects of using a sunblock on the beads.

Materials

5   Ultraviolet Beads
1   Pipe Cleaner
1   Egg Carton
1   Piece of Clear, Plastic Wrap
1   Roll of Masking Tape
1   Pair of Scissors
1   Bottle of Sunblock (optional)
1   Sun (free from dawn until dusk!)

Procedure

1. String the five beads on the pipe cleaner and record the color of each bead, from 1 to 5, in the space provided on the next page.

2. Now, wear the pipe cleaner on your wrist, ankle, toe, or ear and quietly exit outside into the bright sunshine, taking this book and a pencil with you. Record your observations in the data table on the next page.

3. Prepare your egg carton by cutting a two-egg section from the bottom half of the tray. Take the beads off of the pipe cleaner and place two to three beads in each section of your egg carton. Put a piece of clear plastic wrap over one egg section and leave the other open.

4. Head outside once again and expose your beads to the sun. Record observations below.

5. At this time, and with the permission of your folks, you may want to continue exploring the light-blocking abilities by using fabrics, colored paper, different strengths of sunblock, or sunglass lenses.

Data & Observations

Bead #	Color Indoors	Color Outdoors
1		
2		
3		
4		
5		

Bead #	Uncovered	Covered in Plastic
1		
2		
3		
4		
5		

UV Beads

How Come, Huh?

Ultraviolet waves are produced by all stars, including our sun. This light is transmitted through electromagnetic waves, which means that they are measurable waves, usually 0.28 microns to 0.40 microns. The longer waves are generally attributed to causing the production of melanin and a nice tan; the shorter ones rip right through the cell and cream the nuclei. We call that cancer if it gets out of hand.

The ultraviolet beads used in this experiment contain a pigment that absorbs the ultraviolet light from the sun and then radiates it back to us as visible light. The way we think this happens is illustrated below.

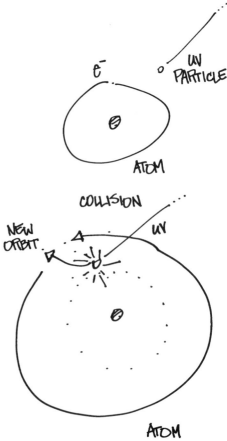

1. A photon of UV light zips away from the sun, travels 92,000,000 miles in about eight minutes, and zips through our atmosphere dodging numerous obstacles to smash into the pigment, which happens to be a molecule, embedded in the bead. You have just added energy to the molecule so something has to change. In this case. . .

2. The collision bumps one of the electrons (illustrated as e-) in the molecule from its regular, comfortable orbit to one that is a little bit farther away from the center of the atom. Translation: The energy from the light was absorbed by and stored in the electron's orbit, until . . .

3. This creates an unstable situation and the electron, wanting to get rid of this extra energy, emits it as light that we see and then returns to its regular orbit, where it continues to hover comfortably around the nucleus. . . until the next UV particle creams the electrons again which bumps an unsuspecting electron into a new orbit . . . and so it goes.

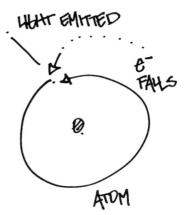

Science Fair Extensions

96. Experiment with different sources of UV light. In addition to the sun try tanning beds, food-heating lamps, various lightbulbs, and UV lamps. Rate the amount of color change and determine how juiced each of these sources are.

97. Repeat the experiment using different brands of sunglasses. Check the glasses that are for sale in the store. Many of them claim that they block harmful UV rays. Place the UV beads in egg cartons and place the sunglass lens over each bead. Record the amount of the color change for each lens and rate them for their effectiveness.

98. Place the beads in the egg carton again and this time cover them with different materials such as black fabric, cellophane, wax paper, aluminum foil, and anything else you can think of to potentially block the UV rays. Record the color changes for each material.

99. The company that manufactures these beads also produces UV sensitive nail polish that changes colors in the sunlight. Design an experiment that uses UV sensitive nail polish.

Solar Cells

The Experiment

So far we have seen light cause a color change in paper, create a rainbow of colors in beads that contain special pigment, the next lab will use a change in state to create an interesting effect, but this lab will demonstrate that energy from either sunlight or artificial light can be captured and converted to electrical energy.

Materials

1   Solar Cell
1   Simple Motor
1   Fan Attachment
2   Wires
1   Lamp, Brighter is Better
1   Sun

Procedure

1. Commercial kits that contain all of the materials mentioned in the Materials section of this lab are readily available or, if you are a do-it-yourself kind of person, everything can be collected or purchased individually from your local hardware and hobby shop.

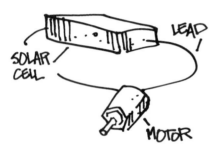

2. Identify the solar cell. It is usually a flat, black rectangle, with a clear, plastic top. Coming off the cell should be two wires or connecting points. This is where you will collect the electricity produced by the cell and use it to run the motor.

3. Hook one wire to each connecting point on the solar cell. Then connect the wires to the two leads that come of the motor. You have just created a very simple series circuit. If you hold the solar cell in the sunshine or under a very bright lamp the motor will begin to spin.

How Come, Huh?

Solar cells are made of a wafer of pure silicon, known as sand to most of us, that has been heated until it melts and then poured into a thin rectangular shape and allowed to cool. When the silicon wafer was being poured, a small amount of the element boron was added to the mix. This gives the wafer a positive electrical charge so they call these "P" (for positive) wafers.

PHOTON OF LIGHT

N LAYER
P LAYER

Next, the engineers making these discs pour a very thin layer of pure silicon over the top of the "P" wafer. This mix contains a different additive, phosphorous, which gives the top half of the sandwich a negative charge. This is called a "N" wafer.

When a photon of light or particle of sunshine hits the solar cell, it bonks the electron from the top layer to the bottom one, producing a flow of electrons from the negative to the positive layers. Viola!, electricity from sunshine. What a country.

Science Fair Extensions

100. Different colors carry different amounts of energy with them, and when they strike the solar cells, that is reflected in the amount of energy that is gathered. Design an experiment and demonstrate that violet, blue, and green wavelengths of light contain more energy than red, orange, and yellow.

A Quanta Puzzle

The Experiment

We saved this experiment for the end of the book since it is probably the grandaddy of all light experiments and has been performed by almost every kid who ever held a hand lens. Light from the sun will be collected and concentrated using the lens. The effect of the concentrated light will allow you to solve the puzzle. The term *quanta* is used to describe units or bundles of light energy.

Materials

1   Quart Jar, Glass, with Metal Lid
1   Hammer
1   Nail, #6
1   12" Piece of Thread
1   Paper Clip
1   Hands Lens, 3" to 5" Diameter
1   Sun

Procedure

1. Remove the metal lid from the jar and punch a hole in the center of it using the hammer and the nail.

2. Feed the thread through the hole and tie the paper clip to the end that will be outside the jar and the nail to the other end.

3. Lower the nail into the jar and screw the lid on. You will want to wind the thread around the paper clip so that the nail is dangling an inch or so above the bottom of the jar.

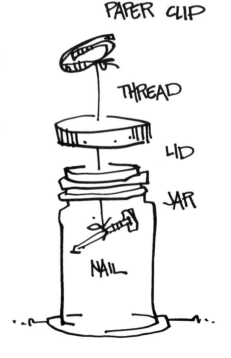

PAPER CLIP

THREAD

LID

JAR

NAIL

4. So, here is the puzzle. Without removing the lid or breaking the jar, figure out a way to "cut" the thread and get the nail to drop to the bottom of the jar. There is a fairly substantial clue in the illustration above.

How Come, Huh?

By focusing the light on the thread, the light energy gets concentrated on one point. As the energy accumulates in this one spot, the temperature of the thread increases until it reaches its kindling point, ignites, and burns. The nail falls to the bottom of the jar because it has gravity pulling on it.

Congratulations! You've either completed the whole book and you now have the knowledge that comes from mucking around with 50 different hands-on activities. Or, you have skipped to the back of the book and you are reading this because you always read the last portion of any book first. Weird but true.

Science Fair Extensions

101. Repeat the experiment using several different kinds of materials to hang the nail: thicker thread, string, fishing line, thin metal wire, human hair, and yarn, for starters. Measure the amount of time it takes for the material to ignite and burn.

If that doesn't tickle your fancy then build and demonstrate a solar oven. As you do the research, you will find that it operates on the same basic principle of gathering and focusing light energy as your hand lens.

Closing Thoughts

Again, congratulations for making it through the entire book. Now that you have a fundamental understanding of light and some of the concepts you can proceed on to more advanced studies and figure out some of the things that we don't know. Among them:

1. Is light a wave or a particle? It behaves like both but we can't nail it down to one or the other. Maybe it's bundles of particles that are traveling together in a wave pattern. But then, what makes the particles of light bundle together in the first place? This is the problem with science. The more questions you ask the more questions appear waiting to be answered.

2. How do we see? No one really knows. They have figured out that light enters the eye but then we die on the vine when that light hits the cones and rods decorating the back of the eye. Do we have small little photovoltaic cells that convert light to electricity so it can travel along the nerve? If so, then how does the electrical impulse in the nerve stimulate the impression of color in the brain?

Maybe you don't want to discover anything but you would rather do some research and invent new stuff.

1. How about glow-in-the-dark lines for the street. Create a mix of paint and phosphorescent pigments, maybe from a mineral you discover, that glows in the dark and allows drivers to better see where it is that they are going at night. It would be great for foggy areas too, and it is a safe bet that your bank account would be a little fatter if you could figure that one out.

2. Perhaps refractive indices could be used for health purposes. Plasma could be collected and the refractive index could be measured against the standards to test for disease.

3. If different levels of light contain different amounts of energy, would it be possible to optimize the production of food in greenhouses by filtering out or enhancing certain wavelengths of light?

4. If polarizing filters can be used to diagnose stress patterns in metal and plastic, how about layers in the eye's sclera. Is stress reflected there? Could it be used as a tool for physiologists who are training world-class athletes to compete? They always say the eyes are the window to the soul. Maybe we could use this concept to solve religious strife in Northern Ireland, the Middle East, India, and Pakistan and anywhere else bigotry and dogma get a leg up on compassion, tolerance, and an appreciation for diversity.

Lots to think about. Hope you enjoyed the book and we would love to pick up with a new topic soon.

Happy Experimenting.

Science Fair Projects
·
A Step-by-Step Guide: From Idea to Presentation

Photon U • Winholtz, Cramer, Twyman, & Hixson

Science Fair Projects

Ah, the impending science fair project. A good science fair project has the following five characteristics:

1. The student must come up with an *original* question.

2. That *original* question must be suited to an experiment in order to provide an answer.

3. The *original* idea is outlined with just one variable isolated.

4. The *original* experiment is performed and documented using the scientific method.

5. A presentation of the *original* idea in the form of a lab write-up and display board is completed.

Science Fair Projects

As simple as science fair versus science project sounds, it gets screwed up millions of times a year by sweet, unsuspecting students who are counseled by sweet, unknowing, and probably just as confused parents.

To give you a sense of contrast we have provided a list of legitimate science fair projects and then reports that do not qualify. We will also add some comments in italics that should help clarify why they do or do not qualify in the science fair project department.

Science Fair Projects

1. Temperature and the amount of time it takes mealworms to change to beetles.

Great start. We have chosen a single variable that is easy to measure: temperature. From this point forward the student can read, explore, and formulate an original question that is the foundation for the project.

A colleague of mine actually did a similar type of experiment for his master's degree. His topic: The rate of development of fly larva in cow poop as a function of temperature. No kidding. He found out that the warmer the temperature of the poop the faster the larva developed into flies.

2. The effect of different concentrations of soapy water on seed germination.

Again, wonderful. Measuring the concentration of soapy water. This leads naturally into original questions and a good project.

3. Crystal size and the amount of sugar in the solution.

This could lead into other factors such as exploring the temperature of the solution, the size of the solution container, and other variables that may affect crystal growth. Opens a lot of doors.

vs. Science Reports

4. Helicopter rotor size and the speed at which it falls.

Size also means surface area, which is very easy to measure. The student who did this not only found the mathematical threshold with relationship to air friction, but she had a ton of fun.

5. The ideal ratio of baking soda to vinegar to make a fire extinguisher.

Another great start. Easy to measure and track, leads to a logical question that can either be supported or refuted with the data.

Each of those topics *measures* one thing such as the amount of sugar, the concentration of soapy water, or the ideal size. If you start with an idea that allows you to measure something, then you can change it, ask questions, explore, and ultimately make a *prediction*, also called a *hypothesis*, and experiment to find out if you are correct. Here are some well-meaning but misguided entries:

Science Reports, <u>not Projects</u>
1. Dinosaurs!

OK, great. Everyone loves dinosaurs but where is the experiment? Did you find a new dinosaur? Is Jurassic Park alive and well, and we are headed there to breed, drug, or in some way test them? Probably not. This was a report on T. rex. Cool, but not a science fair project. And judging by the protest that this kid's mom put up when the kid didn't get his usual "A", it is a safe bet that she put a lot of time in and shared in the disappointment.

More Reports &

2. Our Friend the Sun

Another very large topic, no pun intended. This could be a great topic. Sunlight is fascinating. It can be split, polarized, reflected, refracted, measured, collected, converted. However, this poor kid simply chose to write about the size of the sun, regurgitate facts about its features, cycles, and other astrofacts while simultaneously offending the American Melanoma Survivors Society. Just kidding about that last part.

3. Smokers' Poll

A lot of folks think that they are headed in the right direction here. Again, it depends on how the kid attacks the idea. Are they going to single out race? Heredity? Shoe size? What exactly are they after here? The young lady who did this report chose to make it more of a psychology-studies effort than a scientific report. She wanted to know family income, if they fought with their parents, how much stress was on the job, and so on. All legitimate concerns but not placed in the right slot.

4. The Majestic Moose

If you went out and caught the moose, drugged it to see the side effects for disease control, or even mated it with an elk to determine if you could create an animal that would become the spokesanimal for the Alabama Dairy Farmers' Got Melk? promotion, that would be fine. But, another fact-filled report should be filed with the English teacher.

5. How Tadpoles Change into Frogs

Great start, but they forgot to finish the statement. We know how tadpoles change into frogs. What we don't know is how tadpoles change into frogs if they are in an altered environment, if they are hatched out of cycle, if they are stuck under the tire of an off-road vehicle blatantly driving through a protected wetland area. That's what we want to know. How tadpoles change into frogs, if, when, or under what measurable circumstances.

Now that we have beat the chicken squat out of this introduction, we are going to show you how to pick a topic that can be adapted to become a successful science fair project after one more thought.

One Final Comment

A Gentle Reminder

Quite often I discuss the scientific method with moms and dads, teachers and kids, and get the impression that, according to their understanding, there is one, and only one, scientific method. This is not necessarily true. There are lots of ways to investigate the world we live in and on.

Paleontologists dig up dead animals and plants but have no way to conduct experiments on them. They're dead. Albert Einstein, the most famous scientist of the last century and probably on everybody's starting five of all time, never did experiments. He was a theoretical physicist, which means that he came up with a hypothesis, skipped over collecting materials for things like black holes and space-time continuums, didn't experiment on anything or even collect data. He just went straight from hypothesis to conclusion, and he's still considered part of the scientific community. You'll probably follow the six steps we outline but keep an open mind.

HEY! GOOD NEWS AL, YOU'RE STILL IN THE CLUB.

Project Planner

This outline is designed to give you a specific set of time lines to follow as you develop your science fair project. Most teachers will give you 8 to 11 weeks notice for this kind of assignment. We are going to operate from the shorter time line with our suggested schedule, which means that the first thing you need to do is get a calendar.

A. The suggested time to be devoted to each item is listed in parentheses next to that item. Enter the date of the Science Fair and then, using the calendar, work backward entering dates.

B. As you complete each item, enter the date that you completed it in the column between the goal (due date) and project item.

Goal   Completed   Project Item

1. Generate a Hypothesis (2 weeks)

———— ———— Review Idea Section, pp. 180–183
———— ———— Try Several Experiments
———— ———— Hypothesis Generated
———— ———— Finished Hypothesis Submitted
———— ———— Hypothesis Approved

2. Gather Background Information (1 week)

———— ———— Concepts/Discoveries Written Up
———— ———— Vocabulary/Glossary Completed
———— ———— Famous Scientists in Field

& Time Line

Goal   Completed   Project Item

3. Design an Experiment (1 week)

_____ _____ Procedure Written
_____ _____ Lab Safety Review Completed
_____ _____ Procedure Approved
_____ _____ Data Tables Prepared
_____ _____ Materials List Completed
_____ _____ Materials Acquired

4. Perform the Experiment (2 weeks)

_____ _____ Scheduled Lab Time

5. Collect and Record Experimental Data (part of 4)

_____ _____ Data Tables Completed
_____ _____ Graphs Completed
_____ _____ Other Data Collected and Prepared

6. Present Your Findings (2 weeks)

_____ _____ Rough Draft of Paper Completed
_____ _____ Proofreading Completed
_____ _____ Final Report Completed
_____ _____ Display Completed
_____ _____ Oral Report Outlined on Index Cards
_____ _____ Practice Presentation of Oral Report
_____ _____ Oral Report Presentation
_____ _____ Science Fair Setup
_____ _____ Show Time!

Scientific Method
• Step 1 •
The Hypothesis

Photon U • Winholtz, Cramer, Twyman, & Hixson

The Hypothesis

A hypothesis is an educated guess. It is a statement of what you think will probably happen. It is also the most important part of your science fair project because it directs the entire process. It determines what you study, the materials you will need, and how the experiment will be designed, carried out, and evaluated. Needless to say, you need to put some thought into this part.

There are four steps to generating a hypothesis:

Step One • Pick a Topic
Preferably something that you are interested in studying. We would like to politely recommend that you take a peek at physical science ideas (physics and chemistry) if you are a rookie and this is one of your first shots at a science fair project. These kinds of lab ideas allow you to repeat experiments quickly. There is a lot of data that can be collected, and there is a huge variety to choose from.

If you are having trouble finding an idea, all you have to do is pick up a compilation of science activities (like this one) and start thumbing through it. Go to the local library or head to a bookstore and you will find a wide and ever-changing selection to choose from. Find a topic that interests you and start reading. At some point an idea will catch your eye, and you will be off to the races.

Pick An Idea You Like

We hope you find an idea you like between the covers of this book. But we also realize that 1) there are more ideas about light than we have included in this book, and 2) other kinds of presentations, or methods of writing labs, may be just what you need to trigger a new idea or put a different spin on things. So, without further adieu, we introduce you to several additional titles that may be of help to you in developing a science fair project.

For Older Kids . . .

1. The Magic Wand and other Bright Experiments on Light and Color. Written by Paul Doherty, Don Rathjen, and the Exploratorium Teacher Institute. ISBN 0-471-11515-0 Published by John Wiley & Sons, Inc. 122 pages.

This is a wonderful book from our favorite hands-on science center, the Exploratorium in San Francisco, California. It contains twenty-five science "snacks." These are mini-versions of the larger exhibits that you can find at the Exploratorium. Each snack has been designed by classroom teachers and is kid-tested. In addition to sections giving an overview, a list of materials, assembly instructions (with estimated times), things to do and notice, and questions about what is going on, there is also an etc. section that will give you ideas for developing the lab further. The book also comes with excellent illustrations and photographs to guide you in the construction of the lab.

2. Light Action! Amazing Experiments with Optics. Written by Vicki Cobb. ISBN 0-06-021437-7 Published by HarperCollins. 192 pages.

This is a also an excellent resource. Fifty-seven lab activities are divided up into eleven chapters. This allows you to peruse the ideas and get a good overview of the book. Each section starts with an explanation and some background information, then launches into anywhere from four to eight labs to more fully develop the concepts. There are lots of extension ideas, too.

3. Awesome Experiments with Light & Sound. Written by Michael DiSpezio. ISBN 0-8069-9823-7 Published by Sterling Publishing Co. 160 pages.

This is the most kid-friendly book of the six that we are reviewing. The text is written as if the author were there talking with you. It has cute titles, well-done illustrations, concise directions, and easy-to-understand explanations. The book also covers a wide range of basic ideas on color, light, reflection, mirrors, refraction, and illusions. It has thirty-nine experiments to get you started.

4. Science Projects About Light. Written by Robert Gardner. ISBN 0-89490-529-5 Published by Enslow Publishers, Inc. 128 pages.

Thirty-five lab activities are divided up into five chapters. Although a very good resource, this book tends to follow along the traditional lines of science writing that was characteristic of the 1950s and 1960s. Meaning that it is less kid-friendly in its layout and titles than the other books we are suggesting. On the other side of the coin, the explanations are very thorough and the illustrations are technically precise.

5. The Science Book of Light. Written by Neil Ardley. ISBN 0-15-200577-3 Published by Harcourt, Brace, Jovanovich. 29 pages.

Ten different projects from a kaleidoscope to a box camera to a light-sensitive alfalfa garden. Great springboard for generating ideas.

6. Physics for Every Kid. Written by Janice Van Cleave. ISBN 0-471-52505-7 Published by John Wiley & Sons. 192 pages.

Light is one topic in the field of physics. This book has eleven lab activities devoted to light that touch on several basic ideas. Instructions and explanations are abbreviated compared with other books.

Develop an Original Idea

Step Two • Do the Lab

Choose a lab activity that looks interesting and try the experiment. Some kids make the mistake of thinking that all you have to do is find a lab in a book, repeat the lab, and you are on the gravy train with biscuit wheels. Your goal is to ask an ORIGINAL question, not repeat an experiment that has been done a bazillion times before.

As you do the lab, be thinking not only about the data you are collecting, but of ways you could adapt or change the experiment to find out new information. The point of the science fair project is to have you become an actual scientist and contribute a little bit of new knowledge to the world.

You know that they don't pay all of those engineers good money to sit around and repeat other people's lab work. The company wants new ideas so if you are able to generate and explore new ideas you become very valuable, not only to that company but to society. It is the question-askers that find cures for diseases, create new materials, figure out ways to make existing machines energy efficient, and change the way that we live. For the purpose of illustration, we are going to take a lab from this book and run it through the rest of the process. Turn to page 52 and the lab titled, " Prisms, Water Prisms." The lab uses a tub of water, an ordinary mirror, and light to create a prism that splits the light into the spectrum of a rainbow. Cool. Easy to do. Not expensive and open to all kinds of adaptations, including the four that we provide in the Science Fair Extension section on page 55.

Step Three • Bend, Fold, Spindle, & Mutilate Your Lab
Once you have picked out an experiment, ask if it is possible to do any of the following things to modify it into an original experiment. You want to try and change the experiment to make it more interesting and find out one new, small piece of information.

Heat it	Freeze it	Reverse it	Double it
Bend it	Invert it	Poison it	Dehydrate it
Drown it	Stretch it	Fold it	Ignite it
Split it	Irradiate it	Oxidize it	Reduce it
Chill it	Speed it up	Color it	Grease it
Expand it	Substitute it	Remove it	Slow it down

If you take a look at page 55, that's exactly what we did to the main idea. We took the list of 24 different things that you could do to an experiment—not nearly all of them by the way—and tried a couple of them out on the prism setup.

Double it: 20. Get a second prism and see if you can continue to separate the colors farther by lining up a second prism in the rainbow of the first.

Reduce it: 21. Figure out a way to gather up the colors that have been produced and mix them back together to produce white light again.

Reverse it: 22. Experiment with moving the flashlight and paper closer to the mirror and farther away. Draw a picture and be able to predict what happens to the size and clarity of the rainbow image.

Substitute it: 23. You can also create a rainbow on a sunny day using a garden hose with a fine-spray nozzle attached. Set the nozzle adjustment so that a fine mist is produced and move the mist around in the sunshine until you see the rainbow. This works better if the sun is lower in the sky; late afternoon is best.

Hypothesis Work Sheet

Step Three (Expanded) • *Bend, Fold, Spindle Work Sheet*
This work sheet will give you an opportunity to work through
the process of creating an original idea.

A. Write down the lab idea that you want to mangle.

_____

_____

_____

_____

B. List the possible variables you could change in the lab.
    i. _____
   ii. _____
  iii. _____
   iv. _____
    v. _____

C. Take one variable listed in section B and apply one of the 24
changes listed below to it. Write that change down and state your new
lab idea in the space below. Do that with three more changes.

Heat it	Freeze it	Reverse it	Double it
Bend it	Invert it	Poison it	Dehydrate it
Drown it	Stretch it	Fold it	Ignite it
Split it	Irradiate it	Oxidize it	Reduce it
Chill it	Speed it up	Color it	Grease it
Expand it	Substitute it	Remove it	Slow it down

    i. _____

_____

_____

_____

ii. _____

_____

_____

_____

iii. _____

_____

_____

_____

iv. _____

_____

_____

_____

Step Four • Create an Original Idea— Your Hypothesis

Your hypothesis should be stated as an opinion. You've done the basic experiment, you've made observations, you're not stupid. Put two and two together and make a PREDICTION. Be sure that you are experimenting with just a single variable.

D. State your hypothesis in the space below. List the variable.

i. _____

_____

_____

_____

ii. Variable tested: _____

Sample Hypothesis Work Sheet

On the previous two pages is a work sheet that will help you develop your thoughts and a hypothesis. Here is sample of the finished product to help you understand how to use it.

A. Write down the lab idea that you want to mutilate.
A mirror is placed in a tub of water. A beam of light is focused through the water onto the mirror, producing a rainbow on the wall.

B. List the possible variables you could change in the lab.
   i. **Source of light**
   ii. **The liquid in the tub**
   iii. **The distance from flashlight to mirror**

C. Take one variable listed in section B and apply one of the 24 changes to it. Write that change down and state your new lab idea in the space below.

The shape of the beam of light can be controlled by making and placing cardboard filters over the end of the flashlight. Various shapes such as circles, squares, and slits will produce different quality rainbows.

D. State your hypothesis in the space below. List the variable. Be sure that when you write the hypothesis you are stating an idea and not asking a question.

Hypothesis: The narrower the beam of light the tighter, brighter, and more focused the reflected rainbow will appear.

Variable tested: **The opening on the filter**

Scientific Method
• Step 2 •
Gather Information

Gather Information

Read about your topic and find out what we already know. Check books, videos, the Internet, and movies, talk with experts in the field, and molest an encyclopedia or two. Gather as much information as you can before you begin planning your experiment.

In particular, there are several things that you will want to pay special attention to and that should accompany any good science fair project.

A. Major Scientific Concepts

Be sure that you research and explain the main idea(s) that is / are driving your experiment. It may be a law of physics or chemical rule or an explanation of an aspect of plant physiology.

B. Scientific Words

As you use scientific terms in your paper, you should also define them in the margins of the paper or in a glossary at the end of the report. You cannot assume that everyone knows about geothermal energy transmutation in sulfur-loving bacterium. Be prepared to define some new terms for them. . . and scrub your hands really well when you are done if that is your project.

C. Historical Perspective

When did we first learn about this idea, and who is responsible for getting us this far? You need to give a historical perspective with names, dates, countries, awards, and other recognition.

Building a Research Foundation

1. This sheet is designed to help you organize your thoughts and give you some ideas on where to look for information on your topic. When you prepare your lab report, you will want to include the background information outlined below.

A. *Major Scientific Concepts (Two is plenty.)*

   i. _____

   _____

   _____

   _____

   ii. _____

   _____

   _____

   _____

B. *Scientific Words (No more than 10)*

   i. _____

   ii. _____

   iii. _____

   iv. _____

   v. _____

   vi. _____

   vii. _____

   viii. _____

   ix. _____

   x. _____

C. *Historical Perspective*
   Add this as you find it.

2. There are several sources of information that are available to help you fill in the details from the previous page.

A. *Contemporary Print Resources*
   (Magazines, Newspapers, Journals)
   i. _____
   ii. _____
   iii. _____
   iv. _____
   v. _____
   vi. _____

B. *Other Print Resources*
   (Books, Encyclopedias, Dictionaries, Textbooks)
   i. _____
   ii. _____
   iii. _____
   iv. _____
   v. _____
   vi. _____

C. *Celluloid Resources*
   (Films, Filmstrips, Videos)
   i. _____
   ii. _____
   iii. _____
   iv. _____
   v. _____
   vi. _____

D. Electronic Resources:
   (Internet Website Addresses, DVDs, MP3s)

   i. _____

   ii. _____

   iii. _____

   iv. _____

   v. _____

   vi. _____

   vii. _____

   viii. _____

   ix. _____

   x. _____

E. Human Resources
   (Scientists, Engineers, Professionals, Professors, Teachers)

   i. _____

   ii. _____

   iii. _____

   iv. _____

   v. _____

   vi. _____

You may want to keep a record of all of your research and add it to the back of the report as an Appendix. Some teachers who are into volume think this is really cool. Others, like myself, find it a pain in the tuchus. No matter what you do, be sure to keep an accurate record of where you find data. If you quote from a report word for word, be sure to give proper credit with either a footnote or parenthetical reference, this is very important for credibility and accuracy. This is will keep you out of trouble with plagiarism (copying without giving credit).

Scientific Method
• Step 3 •
Design Your Experiment

Acquire Your Lab Materials

The purpose of this section is to help you plan your experiment. You'll make a map of where you are going , how you want to get there, and what you will take along.

List the materials you will need to complete your experiment in the table below. Be sure to list multiples if you will need more than one item. Many science materials double as household items in their spare time. Check around the house before you buy anything from a science supply company or hardware store. For your convenience, we have listed some suppliers on page 19 of this book.

Material	Qty.	Source	$
1.			
2.			
3.			
4.			
5.			
6.			
7.			
8.			
9.			
10.			
11.			
12.			

Total $_____

Outline Your Experiment

This sheet is designed to help you outline your experiment. If you need more space, make a copy of this page to finish your outline. When you are done with this sheet, review it with an adult, make any necessary changes, review safety concerns on the next page, prepare your data tables, gather your equipment, and start to experiment.

In the space below, list what you are going to do in the order you are going to do it.

i. _____

_____

_____

ii. _____

_____

_____

iii. _____

_____

_____

iv. _____

_____

_____

v. _____

_____

_____

Evaluate Safety Concerns

We have included an overall safety section in the front of this book on pages 16–18, but there are some very specific questions you need to ask, and prepare for, depending on the needs of your experiment. If you find that you need to prepare for any of these safety concerns, place a check mark next to the letter.

_____ *A. Goggles & Eyewash Station*
If you are mixing chemicals or working with materials that might splinter or produce flying objects, goggles and an eyewash station or sink with running water should be available.

_____ *B. Ventilation*
If you are mixing chemicals that could produce fire, smoke, fumes, or obnoxious odors, you will need to use a vented hood or go outside and perform the experiment in the fresh air.

_____ *C. Fire Blanket or Fire Extinguisher*
If you are working with potentially combustible chemicals or electricity, a fire blanket and extinguisher nearby are a must.

_____ *D. Chemical Disposal*
If your experiment produces a poisonous chemical or there are chemical-filled tissues (as in dissected animals), you may need to make arrangements to dispose of the by-products from your lab.

_____ *E. Electricity*
If you are working with materials and developing an idea that uses electricity, make sure that the wires are in good repair, that the electrical demand does not exceed the capacity of the supply, and that your work area is grounded.

_____ *F. Emergency Phone Numbers*
Look up and record the following phone numbers for the Fire Department: _____ , Poison Control: _____ , and Hospital: _____ . Post them in an easy-to-find location.

Prepare Data Tables

Finally, you will want to prepare your data tables and have them ready to go before you start your experiment. Each data table should be easy to understand and easy for you to use.

A good data table has a **title** that describes the information being collected, and it identifies the **variable** and the **unit** being collected on each data line. The variable is *what* you are measuring and the unit is *how* you are measuring it. They are usually written like this:

Variable (unit), or to give you some examples:

Time (seconds)
Distance (meters)
Electricity (volts)

An example of a well-prepared data table looks like the sample below. We've cut the data table into thirds because the book is too small to display the whole line.

Determining the Boiling Point of Compound X_1

Time (min.)	0	1	2	3	4	5	6
Temp. (°C)							

Time (min.)	7	8	9	10	11	12	13
Temp. (°C)							

Time (min.)	14	15	16	17	18	19	20
Temp. (°C)							

Scientific Method
• Step 4 •
Conduct the Experiment

Lab Time

It's time to get going. You've generated a hypothesis, collected the materials, written out the procedure, checked the safety issues, and prepared your data tables. Fire it up. Here's the short list of things to remember as you experiment.

_____ A. *Follow the Procedure, Record Any Changes*
Follow your own directions specifically as you wrote them. If you find the need to change the procedure once you are into the experiment, that's fine; it's part of the process. Make sure to keep detailed records of the changes. When you repeat the experiment a second or third time, follow the new directions exactly.

_____ B. *Observe Safety Rules*
It's easier to complete the lab activity if you are in the lab rather than the emergency room.

_____ C. *Record Data Immediately*
Collect temperatures, distances, voltages, revolutions, and any other variables and immediately record them into your data table. Do not think you will be able to remember them and fill everything in after the lab is completed.

_____ D. *Repeat the Experiment Several Times*
The more data that you collect, the better. It will give you a larger data base and your averages are more meaningful. As you do multiple experiments, be sure to identify each data set by date and time so you can separate them out.

_____ E. *Prepare for Extended Experiments*
Some experiments require days or weeks to complete, particularly those with plants and animals or the growing of crystals. Prepare a safe place for your materials so your experiment can continue undisturbed while you collect the data. Be sure you've allowed enough time for your due date.

Scientific Method
• Step 5 •
Collect and Display Data

Types of Graphs

This section will give you some ideas on how you can display the information you are going to collect as a graph. A graph is simply a picture of the data that you gathered portrayed in a manner that is quick and easy to reference. There are four kinds of graphs described on the next two pages. If you find you need a leg up in the graphing department, we have a book in the series called *Data Tables & Graphing*. It will guide you through the process.

Line and Bar Graphs

These are the most common kinds of graphs. The most consistent variable is plotted on the "x", or horizontal, axis and the more temperamental variable is plotted along the "y", or vertical, axis. Each data point on a line graph is recorded as a dot on the graph and then all of the dots are connected to form a picture of the data. A bar graph starts on the horizontal axis and moves up to the data line.

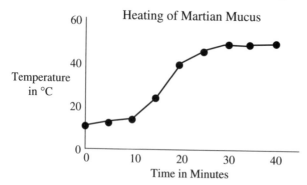

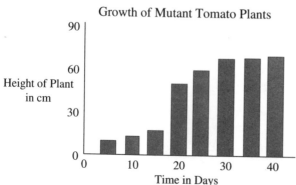

Photon U • Winholtz, Cramer, Twyman, & Hixson

Best Fit Graphs

A best fit graph was created to show averages or trends rather than specific data points. The data that has been collected is plotted on a graph just as on a line graph, but instead of drawing a line from point to point to point, which sometimes is impossible anyway, you just free hand a line that hits "most of the data."

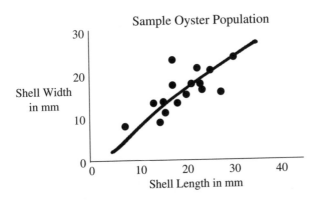

Pie Graphs

Pie graphs are used to show relationships between different groups. All of the data is totaled up and a percentage is determined for each group. The pie is then divided to show the relationship of one group to another.

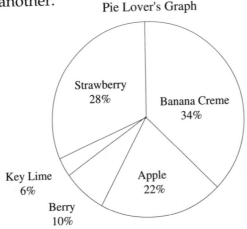

© 2000 • B. K. Hixson

Other Kinds of Data

1. Written Notes & Observations

This is the age-old technique used by all scientists. Record your observations in a lab book. Written notes can be made quickly as the experiment is proceeding, and they can then be expounded upon later. Quite often notes made in the heat of an experiment are revisited during the evaluation portion of the process, and they can shed valuable light on how or why the experiment went the way it did.

2. Drawings

Quick sketches as well as fully developed drawings can be used as a way to report data for a science experiment. Be sure to title each drawing and, if possible, label what it is that you are looking at. Drawings that are actual size are best.

3. Photographs, Videotapes, and Audiotapes

Usually better than drawings, quicker, and more accurate, but you do have the added expense and time of developing the film. However, they can often capture images and details that are not usually seen by the naked eye.

4. The Experiment Itself

Some of the best data you can collect and present is the actual experiment itself. Nothing will speak more effectively for you than the plants you grew, the specimens you collected, or that big pile of tissue that was an armadillo you peeled from the tread of an 18-wheeler.

Scientific Method
· Step 6 ·
Present Your Ideas

Oral Report Checklist

It is entirely possible that you will be asked to make an oral presentation to your classmates. This will give you an opportunity to explain what you did and how you did it. Quite often this presentation is part of your overall score, so if you do well, it will enhance your chances for one of the bigger awards.

To prepare for your oral report, your science fair presentation should include the following components:

Physical Display

_____a.   freestanding display board
          hypothesis
          data tables, graphs, photos, etc.
          abstract (short summary)

_____b.   actual lab setup (equipment)

Oral Report

_____a.   hypothesis or question

_____b.   background information
          concepts
          word definitions
          history or scientists

_____c.   experimental procedure

_____d.   data collected
          data tables
          graphs
          photos or drawings

_____e.   conclusions and findings

_____f.   ask for questions

Set the display board up next to you on the table. Transfer the essential information to index cards. Use the index cards for reference, but do not read from them. Speak in a clear voice, hold your head up, and make eye contact with your peers. Ask if there are any questions before you finish and sit down.

Written Report Checklist

Next up is the written report, also called your lab write-up. After you compile or sort the data you have collected during the experiment and evaluate the results, you will be able to come to a conclusion about your hypothesis. Remember, disproving an idea is as valuable as proving it.

This sheet is designed to help you write up your science fair project and present your data in an organized manner. This is a final checklist for you.

To prepare your write-up, your science fair report should include the following components:

_____ a.　　binder
_____ b.　　cover page, title, & your name
_____ c.　　abstract (one paragraph summary)
_____ d.　　table of contents with page numbers
_____ e.　　hypothesis or question
_____ f.　　background information
　　　　　　　　　concepts
　　　　　　　　　word definitions
　　　　　　　　　history or scientists
_____ g.　　list of materials used
_____ h.　　experimental procedure
　　　　　　　　　written description
　　　　　　　　　photo or drawing of setup
_____ i.　　data collected
　　　　　　　　　data tables
　　　　　　　　　graphs
　　　　　　　　　photos or drawings
_____ j.　　conclusions and findings
_____ k.　　glossary of terms
_____ l.　　references

Display Checklist

2. Prepare your display to accompany the report. A good display should include the following:

Freestanding Display

_____ a.   freestanding cardboard back
_____ b.   title of experiment
_____ c.   your name
_____ d.   hypothesis
_____ e.   findings of the experiment
_____ f.   photo or illustrations of equipment
_____ g.   data tables or graphs

Additional Display Items

_____ h.   a copy of the write-up
_____ i.   actual lab equipment setup

Glossary,
Index,
PDI's Resolved,
A Protractor,
and
More Ideas

Glossary

Amplitude
The size of the wave. The taller the wave the higher the amplitude. If we are talking light, the wave gets brighter; if we are talking sound, the wave gets louder; if we are talking surfing, the wave wins more often.

Angle of Incidence
The incoming angle of light. Measured from a line perpindicular to the reflecting surface from the source of light.

Angle of Reflection
The outgoing angle of light. Measured from a line perpindicular to the reflecting surface to the eye.

Blind Spot
The area in the back of the eye where the optic nerve connects to the tapetum. There are no cones or rods located there, so if a light image strikes that area you do not perceive it in your brain.

Crest
The top of the wave.

Critical Angle
The angle that a ray of light, traveling between a denser material, like water, to a less dense material, like air must strike to pass from one material into the other. If the ray strikes at an angle less than the critical angle, it will pass into the more dense material. If it strikes it at more than the critical angle, it will be reflected back into the material.

Diffraction of Light
The splitting or dividing of white light into the different colors of the rainbow. This can be done with a prism, a drop of water, or a diffraction grating.

Glossary

Diffraction Grating
A thin piece of plastic film that has lots of vertical cuts on the surface. As white light strikes the surface, it is split into wavelengths producing bands of color that can help identify a material.

Electromagnetic Spectrum
The United Nations of waves. Everything from slow-moving radio waves with really long frequencies to X and gamma rays that have extremely high frequencies. Visible light is a skinny band in the middle of the pig pile.

Eye
Greeting or acknowledgment by a person of Scottish origin.

Images
Real • What you see is what you get. If you look at the image of a candle flame on the back of a balloon, that is a real image.
Virtual • It looks like its there, but it really isn't. If you look at the image of yourself in the mirror, you are percieving the image, particularly the distance, but it is not really there.

Index of Refraction
The angle that light is bent when it enters a material that is more or less dense than the material it is traveling in. It is calculated by measuring the change in the speed of light through the material.

Interference
Constructive • When two waves collide in a way that they add together and enhance one another.
Destructive • When two waves collide in a way that they wipe each other out, effectively removing that color from view.
Patterns • The changing colors and patterns that are produced when objects that have wave interference are bent, twisted, or otherwise produce a changing wave pattern.

Glossary

Lenses
Concave • A lens that is curved inward, like a cave. Light images are reflected and inverted when they hit this surface.

Convex • A lens that is curved outward and bends light outward when it strikes the surface.

Polarizing • A colored lens that only allows light traveling in a single plane to pass through.

Line Spectrum
The fingerprint of light bands, red, orange, yellow, and so on that are produced when light enters and is split by diffraction grating.

Opaque
This term describes a material that will not allow light to travel through it.

Persistence of Vision
The afterimage that lingers in the mind once the real image has moved. This phenomenon allows us to watch cartoons and movies as well as use novelty items like zoetropes and flip books.

Prism
An equilateral-triangle bar that splits light into the colors of the rainbow.

Reflector
A material that bounces or reflects some or all of the light that strikes its surface.

Spectroscope
An instrument with a narrow slit in one end and diffraction grating in the other. As the light enters the spectroscope, it is split into individual bands of color. These patterns of color are used to identify the material that produced the light.

Glossary

Total Internal Reflection
If light strikes the interface between two different materials at an angle greater than the critical angle, it will be reflected back into that material. This is the principle that drives fiber-optic cables and what happens to light that travels through a beam of water.

Translucent
This describes any material that will allow some light to pass through it, but the pathway is very diffuse. Frosted glass is an excellent example, so are most plastics.

Transparent
This term describes any material that will allow light to pass through it, without much distortion at all. The image is clear and easily discernible.

Visual Spectrum
The colors that we see. This is a very narrow band of the total electromagnetic spectrum that is found right in the middle of the known frequencies.

Waves
A term describing the path of movement that a particle of light may take from one point to another.

Wavelength
How waves are measured. A complete wave looks like a sideways S. The distance between the crests or troughs of two consecutive waves is defined as the wavelength, is measured in nanometers, and is defined as the wavelength. This measurement classifies the wave as a radio wave, infrared wave, visual spectrum wave, ultraviolet wave, X ray, or gamma ray.

Index

Index

Lenses
    concave, 97–105
    convex, 29, 97–105
    model, 28, 32–37
    polarizing, 86, 89, 92, 94
Mirrors, 127, 130, 132
Opaque, 73, 76–78
Optical Density, 95, 118
Optical Illusion, 114, 118, 147, 149, 151–156
Perceived Depth Image, 156
Peripheral Vision, 42
Persistence of Vision, 149
Prism
    glass, 52–55
    water, 52–55
Pupil, 48
Reflection, 127, 130, 137
Shadow, 73
Spectroscope, 56, 80, 83
    homemade, 83
Stereoscopic Vision, 50
Total Internal Reflection, 135, 137
Translucent, 76–78, 116
Transparent, 76–78, 116
Visual Purple, 48–49
Visual Spectrum, 59
Ultraviolet, 159, 161
    beads, 161
    images, 159
    light, 160
Wavelength, 23, 24, 64, 92
Waves, 22, 88, 140

Answer to PDI

* The perceived depth image, found on page 156, is a series of stars forming an arc that rises up toward you out of the page. It looks something like this:

Protractor

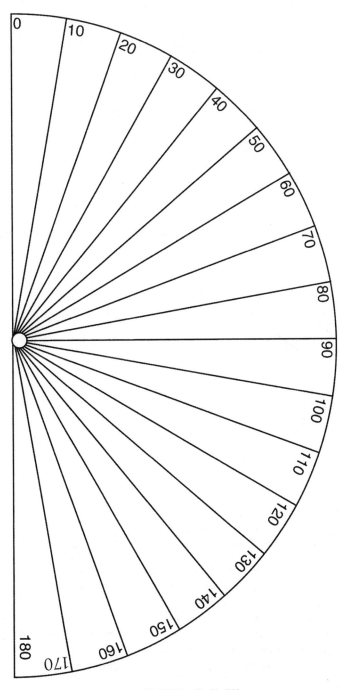

More Physics Books

Catch a Wave

40 hands-on lab activities that sound off on the topic of noise, vibration, waves, the Doppler Effect and associated ideas.

Thermodynamic Thrills

35 hands-on lab activities that investigate heat via conduction, convection, radiation, specific heat, and temperature.

Relatively Albert

50 hands-on lab activities that explore the world of mechanics, forces, gravity, and Newton's three laws of motion.

Gravity Works

50 hands-on lab activities from the world of things that fly. Air, air pressure, Bernoulli's law, and all things that fly, float, or glide are explored.

Electron Herding 101

50 hands-on lab activities that introduce static electricity, circuit electricity and include a number of fun, and very easy-to-build projects.

Opposites Attract

35 hands-on lab activities that delve into the world of natural and man-made magnets as well as the characteristics of magnetic attraction.